JAPANESE WORDS AND THEIR USES

JAPANESE WORDS
AND
THEIR USES

by Akira Miura

CHARLES E. TUTTLE COMPANY
Rutland · Vermont : Tokyo · Japan

REPRESENTATIVES

For the British Isles & Continental Europe:
Simon & Schuster International Group, *London*

For Australasia:
Bookwise International
1 Jeanes Street, Beverley, 5009, South Australia

Published by the Charles E. Tuttle Company, Inc.
of Rutland, Vermont & Tokyo, Japan
with editorial offices at
Suido 1-chome, 2–6, Bunkyo-ku, Tokyo

Library of Congress Catalog Card No. 82–51099
International Standard Book No. 0–8048–1386–8

First printing, 1983
Fourth printing, 1987

Printed in Japan

TABLE OF CONTENTS

PREFACE

I have been teaching Japanese to Americans for more than seventeen years. During that time I have observed many errors in Japanese made by my American students. Most of these errors are attributable to the students' insufficient mastery of Japanese grammar (for example, their inability to inflect verbs correctly), but there are also a large number of errors that are basically due to vocabulary problems.

When the American student of Japanese first comes across a new Japanese word, it is usually introduced with the English "equivalent"; e.g., *atatakai* is matched up with "warm." The student is therefore very likely to conclude that there is in fact a one-to-one correspondence between the two words, and he does indeed start using *atatakai,* for example, in all situations where "warm" would be appropriate in English. He might thus say to a Japanese friend in the midst of summer, with the mercury hitting the mid-80s Fahrenheit, *Kyoo wa atatakai desu nee* meaning "It's warm today, isn't it!" That would really baffle the Japanese friend because, in Japanese, temperatures that high are not *atatakai* but *atsui* "hot." *Atatakai* most aptly describes a nice spring day that arrives after the cold months of winter.

Japanese Words and Their Uses is a reference book that provides help for American students of Japanese, especially those at the elementary and intermediate levels, by explaining approximately three hundred words and phrases. It explains not only how they are used but also how they should *not* be used, contrasting them as often as possible with their English "equivalents." Many of the errors cited in this book have actually been committed by my own students (although they are not always quoted verbatim).

There are just as many synonyms in Japanese as there are in English, and they create serious problems for students of Japanese. For example, both *omou* and *kangaeru* are usually introduced in textbooks as "to think" without adequate explanation of the difference between them. Therefore, a number of near synonyms such as *omou* and *kangaeru* have been included in the book, with sample sentences as well as explanations of their differences.

If American and other English-speaking students of Japanese can find in this book solutions to some of their problems, I will be more than happy. It is also my hope that teachers of Japanese working with English-speaking students may find helpful information in it.

I would like to express my appreciation to Professor Matsuo Soga, of the University of British Columbia, and to Ricky Davis, a graduate student in Japanese at the University of Wisconsin, for reading my manuscript painstakingly and making suggestions to improve it. Thanks are also due to my wife, Charlotte, who proofread the final draft for me.

—AKIRA MIURA

EXPLANATORY NOTES

ARRANGEMENT OF ENTRIES

The main text of this book consists of a list of Japanese terms, alphabetized by their romanized forms, with commentaries. Each entry heading gives the term in romanization, and in Japanese *kanji* (ideographic characters) and/or *kana* (syllabics), then one or more English "equivalents." The kanji usage is kept within the Joyo Kanji, and limited to those widely in use. There follows a detailed explanation of the term's usage.

TERMINOLOGY

Since this book is meant not as a scholarly treatise but rather as a reference book for elementary- and intermediate-level students, the number of technical terms has been kept to a minimum. The few that are used are by and large from Eleanor Harz Jorden's *Beginning Japanese* and/or Matsuo Soga's and Noriko Matsumoto's *Foundations of Japanese Language*.

Adjectives. Japanese adjectives are inflected words that end in *-ai, -ii, -ui,* or *-oi. Hayai* "fast," *ookii* "large," *furui* "old," and *hiroi* "wide," for example, are adjectives. The *-ku* form of an adjective (e.g., *hayaku*) is referred to as the adverbial form.

Nouns. Japanese nouns are noninflected words that can occur before *desu* to constitute complete utterances. *Hon* "book," *eiga* "movie," and *gaijin* "foreigner," are nouns.

Na-nouns. *Na*-nouns are like nouns in that they may occur with *desu* to form complete sentences. When a *na*-noun is used to modify a noun, however, *na* must be inserted in between (e.g., *kirei na hana* "a beautiful flower"), whereas a genuine noun takes *no* instead (e.g., *Tookyoo no chizu* "a map of Tokyo"). *Na*-nouns are known by different names in different textbooks, e.g., "nominal adjectives," "*na*-adjectives," and "pseudoadjectives." Examples of *na*-nouns are *kirei* "beautiful," *genki* "healthy," and *shitsurei* "rude."

Verbs. Japanese verbs are inflected words that take *-masu* in the formal nonpast and *-mashita* in the formal past. *Iku* "to go," *kuru* "to come," and *taberu* "to eat," for example, are verbs.

Stative verbs. Verbs that express states rather than actions are stative verbs. They are such verbs as "to be" and "to have" in English and *iru* "(someone) is (somewhere)" and *aru* "(something) is (somewhere)" in Japanese.

Punctual verbs. Verbs representing actions or occurrences that take place without duration over time are punctual verbs. *Shinu* "to die," *tsuku* "to arrive," and *kekkon-suru* "to get married" are examples of this type.

Potential forms of verbs. Potential forms are forms that mean "can do such and such" or "such and such can be done." *Yomeru,* for example, is the potential form of *yomu* "to read" and means "can read" or "can be read."

Particles. Japanese particles are uninflected words that occur within or at the end of a sentence. They generally do not begin an utterance. When they occur within a sentence, they relate what precedes (whether a word, a phrase, or a clause) to what follows. (For this reason, particles are sometimes called "relationals" instead.) Examples of this type are *wa, ga, o,* and *to.* Particles that occur at the end of a sentence are called sentence particles, and they make the sentence interrogative, exclamatory, emphatic, etc. Examples of this type are *ka, nee,* and *yo.*

JAPANESE ACCENT

Accent marks are used in this book. They are, as a rule, used in the entry headings only, e.g., o͞okiī.

Unlike English, which has a stress accent, Japanese has a pitch accent. In Japanese words, each syllable is spoken either high or low. If the first syllable is low, the second is always high, and if the first syllable is high, the second is always low. In this book, the mark ⌐ indicates a rise in pitch, and the mark ⌐ indicates a fall in pitch. The syllable followed by ⌐ is always the accented syllable. For example, o͞okiī, a four-syllable word, should be pronounced low–high–high–low, and KI, the last syllable before the fall, is the accented syllable. Some words are left completely unmarked, e.g., KIMONO. Unmarked words are accentless (or unaccented) words, i.e., words that do not have a fall in pitch. In accentless words, the first syllable is always low, but the remaining syllables are all high, and there is no fall in pitch even when the words are followed by a particle. For example, *kimono wa* is pronounced

mono wa
ki

Words that end with an accented syllable (e.g., JIBIKI) have the same accent pattern as accentless words when pronounced by themselves, but when they are followed by a particle, a difference emerges. For example, JIBIKI (accented) and KIMONO (accentless) have exactly the same pitch pattern when pronounced alone, but when followed by a particle (e.g., *wa*), they are pronounced differently, as follows:

$$\textit{jibiki wa} \rightarrow \textit{ji} \quad \begin{matrix} \textit{biki} \\ \textit{wa} \end{matrix}$$

$$\textit{kimono wa} \rightarrow \textit{ki} \quad \begin{matrix} \textit{mono wa} \\ \end{matrix}$$

Note that *wa* in *jibiki wa* is low while *wa* in *kimono wa* is high.

ROMANIZATION

The system of romanization used in this book is the popular Hepburn system. There are, however, some points that should be mentioned. In this book, ん is always written *n*, even before *m, p,* and *b;* when *n* should be pronounced independently of a vowel or *y* that follows it, an apostrophe is inserted in between, as in *hon'ya* "bookstore"; long vowels are generally indicated by doubling the vowels (e.g., *aa* and *oo*) instead of by using macrons. Long vowels are not indicated in the Bibliography; the honorific prefix *o-* is not set off.

OTHER CONVENTIONS

An asterisk is used in this book to mark ungrammatical or incorrect utterances. A question mark at the beginning of a sentence indicates unnaturalness or awkwardness. Brackets in Japanese sentences indicate optional portions, while in English translations they show implied meaning.

JAPANESE WORDS AND THEIR USES

ABUNAI 危ない dangerous

Abunai most often means "dangerous, risky, hazardous."
(1) **Yopparai-unten wa abunai.**
    Drunk driving is dangerous.
(2) **Kodomo no matchi-asobi wa abunai.**
    Children's playing with matches is hazardous.

Abunai! may be used as an exclamation in situations where "Look out!" or "Watch out!" would be called for in English. For example, if you see someone walking into the path of an oncoming car, you shout out, *Abunai!* Other examples of adjectives used to give warning are *Urusai!* and *Yakamashii!* (lit., "[You are] noisy!"), both meaning "Be quiet!" or "Shut up!" (see URUSAI).

AGARU 上がる to go up

The basic meaning of *agaru* is "to go up."
(1) **Mata gasorin no nedan ga agatta.**
    The price of gasoline has gone up again.

Entering a Japanese-style house as a guest is also *agaru* because it is an act of "going up." When you enter a Japanese home, you first step into the *genkan,* or vestibule. There you take off your shoes and *take a step up* to the floor level of the house. The act of stepping into the vestibule is *hairu* "to go in," but the act of stepping up to the floor level of the house is *agaru* "to take a step up." That is why the Japanese host says to a visitor
(2) **Doozo oagari kudasai.**
    Please come in (lit., step up).
Sentence (3) below therefore sounds extremely strange.
(3) *Nihonjin wa uchi ni hairu mae ni kutsu o nugimasu.*

The Japanese take off their shoes before going into the house.

Agaru has to be used in this context. Otherwise sentence (3) would describe someone taking off his shoes outside the front door!

AISURU 愛する **to love**

The noun *ai* "love" and its verbal counterpart, *aisuru* "to love," are both written expressions. Although some young lovers nowadays may use such words of endearment as *Aishite-iru yo* (men's speech) and *Aishite-iru wa* (women's speech) to mean "I love you," such sentences still sound stilted because the verb *aisuru* is rarely used in speech. *Kimi ga suki da* (men's speech) and *Anata ga suki yo* (women's speech) also mean "I love you." The versions containing *suki* (see SUKI) are more conversational and are perhaps more frequently used in speech than the versions with *aisuru*. As Donald Keene (p. 156) wisely points out, however, the most typically Japanese expression of love has been silence (although, in the rapidly changing society of contemporary Japan, this tradition too may be on its way out).

AKACHAN 赤ちゃん **baby**

Akachan is normally a word for someone else's baby

(1) **Otaku no akachan wa hontoo ni ogenki soo desu nee.**
     Your baby really looks healthy, doesn't he/she!

Although some Japanese, especially women, use the word to refer to their own babies, the practice, in my opinion, is in poor taste. The word to be used in that case is *akanboo*.

(2) **Kyoo wa uchi no akanboo no tanjoobi na n desu.**
Today is my baby's birthday.

AKEMASHITE OMEDETOO GOZAIMASU 明けまして
おめでとうございます **Happy New Year!**

When a New Year draws near, English speakers still new in Japan often ask their Japanese friends how to say "Happy New Year!" in Japanese. The answer is almost always *Akemashite omedetoo gozaimasu* (or its equivalent *Shinnen omedetoo gozaimasu*). Having received this answer, these English speakers practice hard to memorize this long salutation and, after finally learning it, they try it on their Japanese associates—most likely toward the end of December. Unfortunately this Japanese greeting may not be used until New Year's Day since it literally means "[The New Year] having begun, this is indeed a happy occasion." This contrasts with the English salutation "Happy New Year!" which is an abbreviation of "I wish you a happy New Year" and may therefore be used before the arrival of the New Year. The expression to be used before the old year expires is *Yoi otoshi o omukae kudasai* "May you see in a good year!" However, this is a rather formal salutation and is rarely used among close friends. There is regrettably no informal equivalent, except for the shorter form *Yoi otoshi o,* which is sometimes used.

In America, New Year's wishes are exchanged with vigor at 12 midnight among those present at New Year's Eve parties. After that, however, "Happy New Year!" is, as it were, put away in mothballs. In Japan, *Akemashite omedetoo gozaimasu* is heard at least through the first week of January, and sometimes as late as the middle of the month.

AMAI 甘い sweet

Amai primarily means "sweet in taste."
(1) **amai keeki (chokoreeto, kyandee, etc.)**
    sweet cake (chocolate, candy, etc.)
  Used figuratively, *amai* can mean "indulgent, lenient" or "overly optimistic."
(2) **amai oya**
    indulgent parents
(3) **amai ten**
    lenient grades (*or* marks)
(4) **amai kangae**
    an overly optimistic view
  Unlike English "sweet," *amai* cannot mean "amiable" or "kind." In English, calling someone a sweet person would be complimentary. In Japanese, on the other hand, *amai hito,* if it means anything at all, can only be interpreted as either "an indulgent person" or "an overly optimistic person.'

AMARI あまり too, excessively

Amari means "too" in the sense of "excessively." The word mainly appears in negative sentences.
(1) **Kyoo wa amari samuku nai.**
    It is not too cold today.
(2) **Koko wa amari shizuka ja nai.**
    It is not too quiet here.
(3) **Watashi wa amari nomimasen.**
    I don't drink too much.
  Amari may be used in the affirmative if it appears in a dependent clause.

(4) **Amari nomu to byooki ni narimasu yo.**
    If you drink too much, you'll get sick.
(5) **Kami[noke] ga amari nagai kara, katte-moratta hoo ga ii yo.**
    Your hair is too long; you should get a haircut.
(6) **Koko wa amari shizuka de sabishii-gurai desu.**
    It's so quiet here that it almost makes one feel lonely.

The following sentences, which are independent affirmative sentences, are ungrammatical.

(7) *Anata wa amari nomimasu.*
    You drink too much.
(8) *Kaminoke ga amari nagai.*
    Your hair is too long.
(9) *Koko wa amari shizuka desu.*
    It's too quiet here.

To express the ideas of the English translations of sentences (7) through (9) above, use -*sugiru*.

(10) **Anata wa nomi-sugimasu.**
    You drink too much.
(11) **Kaminoke ga naga-sugiru.**
    Your hair is too long.
(12) **Koko wa shizuka-sugimasu.**
    It's too quiet here.

Amari may be used in combination with -*sugiru* words also, without changing the meaning.

(13) **Anata wa amari nomi-sugimasu.**
    You drink too much. (same as 10 above)
(14) **Kaminoke ga amari naga-sugiru.**
    Your hair is too long. (same as 11)
(15) **Koko wa amari shizuka-sugimasu.**
    It's too quiet here. (same as 12)

Anmari is a more colloquial version of *amari*. There is no difference in meaning between the two.

⌐ ¬
ANATA あなた **you**

Anata "you (singular)" has a very limited use. In fact, long conversations between two people may be carried on without *anata* being used even once. In contexts where it is clear that the speaker is talking about the hearer, no verbal reference to the latter is usually made.

(1) **Ogenki desu ka.**
    Are you well?

Even when reference to the hearer is verbalized, *anata* is usually avoided. The speaker is much more likely to use the hearer's name with *-san* attached.

(2) **Tanaka-san wa moo ano eiga o mimashita ka.** (speaking to Tanaka)
    Have you (lit., Mr./Mrs./Miss Tanaka) seen that movie yet?

If the speaker is lower in status than the hearer, he uses the latter's title as a term of address.

(3) **Sensei wa koohii to koocha to dochira ga osuki desu ka.** (speaking to one's teacher)
    Which do you (lit., teacher) like better, coffee or tea?

(4) **Kachoo wa ashita gorufu o nasaimasu ka.** (speaking to one's section chief)
    Are you (lit., section chief) playing golf tomorrow?

Anata is perhaps used more often by women than by men. Women say *anata,* for example, to their husbands or close friends.

(5) **Anata doo suru.**
    What are you going to do?

Anata has a more informal and less polite variant, *anta.* It is wise to avoid using this altogether since it is difficult, especially for nonnative speakers, to determine when it can be safely used. (See also KIMI. For a detailed discussion of

Japanese terms of address, see Suzuki, Ch. 5 "Words for Self and Others.")

ANE 姉 older sister

Ane is a generic term for older sisters. It is used by adults, especially in writing, to refer to older sisters in general.

(1) **Nihon de wa ane wa imooto yori meue da.**
   In Japan, older sisters are of higher status than younger sisters.

This use of *ane,* however, is generally restricted to written Japanese. In conversational Japanese, *onee-san* is the norm.

(2) **Nihon de wa onee-san wa imooto yori meue da.**
   (same meaning as 1 above)

   When talking to an outsider, an adult refers to his own older sister as *ane.*

(3) **Kinoo ane ga kekkon-shimashita.**
   My older sister got married yesterday.

   An adult talking to an outsider about the latter's older sister or someone else's uses *onee-san.*

(4) **Kinoo onee-san ga kekkon-nasatta soo desu nee.**
   I hear your older sister got married yesterday.

(5) **Yoshida-san no onee-san wa eigo no sensei desu.**
   Mr. Yoshida's older sister is an English teacher.

   An adult also uses *onee-san* in addressing his own older sister or in talking to his family about his older sister.

(6) **Onee-san, chotto matte.**
   lit., Big sister, wait a minute.

(7) **Onee-san doko.** (speaking to one's family)
   lit., Where's big sister?

   (In corresponding situations in English, one would of course use the sister's given name.)

The use of *ane* is restricted to adult speakers. Children say *onee-san* in referring not only to older sisters in general or someone else's older sister, but to their own as well, whether they are talking to an outsider or a member of their own family.

Onee-san has variants such as *nee-san, onee-chan,* and *nee-chan* (the last two being used mainly by children). *Ane* also has a variant (though perhaps not a very common one), *aneki,* which is used by young men in informal conversations, primarily with outsiders.

Since *ane* sounds very similar to *ani* "older brother," the two words must be pronounced carefully and distinctly to avoid confusion. *Ane* is accentless while *ani* is accented on the first syllable (see A̅NI. For a detailed discussion of family terms, see Suzuki, Ch. 5 "Words for Self and Others").

A̅NI 兄 older brother

Ani "older brother" is the male counterpart of *ane* "older sister." What can be said of *ane* (see ANE) on the female side, therefore, can be said of *ani* on the male side. One should remember the following parallels: *ani* corresponds to *ane* in usage; *onii-san* corresponds to *onee-san; nii-san, onii-chan,* and *nii-chan* correspond to *nee-san, onee-chan,* and *nee-chan,* respectively; and *aniki* corresponds to *aneki* (though *aniki* is much more commonly used than the latter).

A̅OI 青い blue

The adjective *aoi* and its nominal counterpart, *ao,* cover a wider range of color than does "blue," since the Japanese word may also refer to the range of color that one would call "green" in English. Though *aoi* normally means "blue," it can indicate "green" in reference to a limited number of items (though *midori* "green" is also acceptable), especially vegetation, as in *aoi shiba* "green grass," *aoi kusaki* "green vegetation," and *ao-shingoo* "green traffic light." Centuries ago, according to Ikegami (p. 16), the use of *ao* for green was even more extensive than now; nowadays, however, in the sense of "green," *midori* is becoming more popular.

Aoi also means "pale" in reference to a person's complexion.

(1) **Suzuki-san doo shita n deshoo ka. Aoi kao o shite-imasu yo.**

I wonder what's happened to Mr. Suzuki. He looks pale.

In this case, no other color word may replace *aoi*.

ARE あれ that

In Japanese, there are two words corresponding to the English demonstrative "that" as in "That is a park." They are *are* and *sore*. The difference between these two Japanese demonstratives when used with reference to visible things is that *are* is for something removed from both the speaker and the addressee while *sore* refers to something removed from the speaker but close to the addressee. Suppose you are talking to Mr. Suzuki and want to refer to a book that he is holding in his hand. Then use *sore,* as in

(1) **Sore wa nan no hon desu ka.**

What book is that?

On the other hand, if you and Mr. Suzuki want to talk

about a building seen in the distance, you use *are* and say, for example,

(2) **Are wa nan no tatemono deshoo ne.**
I wonder what building that is.

When *are* and *sore* are used as prenoun modifiers, they become *ano* and *sono,* as in *ano pen* "that pen" and *sono hon* "that book," but the semantic difference between *ano* and *sono* remains parallel to that between *are* and *sore*.

Since, in Japanese, words normally do not differ in form whether they are singular or plural, *are* and *sore* can mean "those" instead of "that." The same is true of *ano* and *sono*.

With reference to something that is not visible to either the speaker or the hearer at the time of speech, *are* and *sore* are used as follows. *Are* is used "when the speaker knows that the hearer, as well as the speaker himself, knows the referent" whereas *sore* is used "either when the speaker knows the referent but thinks that the hearer does not or when the speaker does not know the referent" (Kuno, p. 283). Compare the following examples:

(3) A: **Kinoo Sutaa Woozu to iu eiga o mimashita yo.**
    Yesterday I saw a movie called *Star Wars*.
  B: **Are** (not **Sore*) **wa omoshiroi eiga desu nee.**
    That's a fun movie, isn't it?

(4) A: **Kinoo Roshia-eiga o mimashita yo.**
    Yesterday I saw a Russian movie.
  B: **Sore** (not **Are*) **wa donna eiga deshita ka.**
    What kind of movie was that?

In (3), speaker B has already seen the movie, so he refers to it as *are*. In (4), on the other hand, speaker B does not know what movie speaker A is talking about, so he uses *sore* instead.

⌐⌐
ARIGATOO GOZAIMASU　ありがとうございます
Thank you

The Japanese equivalent of "Thank you" has variants depending on the tense. If you want to thank someone for something that he is doing, is going to do, or repeatedly does for you, you say *Arigatoo gozaimasu.* To thank someone for what he has already done for you, however, you say *Arigatoo gozaimashita.* For example, if someone has just invited you to a party that is to take place next week, you say *Arigatoo gozaimasu.* After the party, however, you say *Arigatoo gozaimashita,* meaning "Thank you for what you *did* for me." Likewise, as you accept a present from someone, you say *Arigatoo gozaimasu,* but next time you see him, you thank him again by saying *Arigatoo gozaimashita.* The difference in usage between these two forms remains even when *doomo* "very much" is added for emphasis. *Doomo arigatoo gozaimasu* functions like *Arigatoo gozaimasu,* and *Doomo arigatoo gozaimashita* like *Arigatoo gozaimashita,* except that the versions with *doomo* are more polite than the ones without.

The informal version *Arigatoo* (without *gozaimasu* or *gozaimashita*) may be used regardless of the time of the event for which you wish to show gratitude. This version, however, cannot be used when speaking to someone higher in status. Since it is difficult for nonnative speakers of Japanese to determine who is higher or lower than they are, the safest thing would be to use *Arigatoo* only when talking to a child. Otherwise, use the full form *Arigatoo gozaimasu* (or *gozaimashita*), or simply *Doomo.*

Unlike "Thank you," *Arigatoo gozaimasu* and its variants may not be used in response to compliments. If someone compliments you for your "excellent Japanese," for example, say *Mada dame desu* "It's still no good." Thanking someone for a compliment, to the Japanese way of thinking, is like admitting you deserve the compliment; it is therefore an act of conceit.

ARU ある，在る **to be;** 有る **to have**

Aru means "to be" in the sense of "to exist." As a rule, the verb is used with inanimate subjects (including plants).

(1) **Ishii-san no uchi wa Nagoya ni aru.**
    Mr. Ishii's house is in Nagoya.
(2) **Go-gatsu no dai-isshuu ni wa kyuujitsu ga futsu-ka aru.**
    There are two national holidays during the first week of May.

Aru may also be used with reference to animate beings, particularly family members, or other humans comparable to family members, e.g., friends and guests. *X ga aru* in this usage is very much like *X o motte-iru* "to have X" in meaning, as in the following examples:

(3) **Watashi wa kyoodai ga go-nin aru.**
    I have five siblings.
(4) **Yamamoto-san wa kodomo ga san-nin aru soo da.**
    I hear Mr. Yamamoto has three children.
(5) **Ii tomodachi ga aru kara ii desu ne.**
    Isn't it good that you have nice friends!

Although to signify the existence of animate beings, *iru* (see IRU) is the verb that is usually used (e.g., *Asoko ni inu ga iru* "There's a dog over there"), *aru* is sometimes used, especially (a) if the subject is not a specific person or a specific animal, (b) if where the subject exists is irrelevant, and (c) if the noun signaling the subject is preceded by a relative clause, as in

(6) **Yoku benkyoo-suru gakusei mo aru shi, asonde bakari iru gakusei mo aru.**

There are students who study hard and there are students who fool around all the time.

There is another important use of *aru:* to refer to happenings or events.

(7) **Konban hanabi ga aru soo da.**

I hear there will be fireworks tonight.

In this case, *aru* does not indicate existence, but rather refers to an event. When a location is mentioned, therefore, the particle *de* (not *ni*) is required.

(8) **Konban Ryoogoku de hanabi ga aru soo da.**

I hear there will be fireworks at Ryogoku tonight.

Compare this with sentence (1), where *ni* is used to indicate location.

ARUKU 歩く **to walk**

Aruku means "to walk."

(1) **Ano hito wa aruku no ga hayai desu nee.**

He walks fast, doesn't he!

When the destination is mentioned, the particle preceding *aruku* should be *made* "up to." When *e* or *ni,* both meaning "to," is used, the verb is changed to *aruite iku* (lit., "to go walking") or *aruite kuru* (lit., "to come walking").

(2) **Itsumo gakkoo made arukimasu.**

I always walk to school.

(3) **Itsumo gakkoo e (or ni) aruite-ikimasu.**

I always go to school on foot.

When the place along or through which the act of walking takes place is mentioned, *aruku* is preceded by the particle *o*.

(4) **Asoko o aruite-iru no wa dare deshoo.**

I wonder who that person is who is walking over there
(lit. along that place).

Other verbs of motion such as *iku* "to go" and *kuru* "to
come" are also used with *o* in comparable situations.

When walking takes place up or down a steep incline
(e.g., stairs), *aruku* has to be either replaced by another verb
(such as *noboru* "to climb up") or changed to the -*te* form
and followed by another verb (e.g., *aruite noboru*). In the
following example (5), therefore, (a) is incorrect while (b)
and (c) are correct.

(5) **kaidan o** | (a) *aruku
             | (b) **noboru**
             | (c) **aruite noboru**

to climb (*or* walk up) the stairs

Unlike "walk," *aruku* is normally not used in the sense
of "to take a stroll." Sentence (6) is therefore wrong for the
meaning intended.

(6) **Kyoo wa tenki ga ii kara issho ni arukimashoo.*

Since it's such a beautiful day today, let's take a walk
together.

Arukimashoo in this case should be replaced by *sanpo-
shimashoo* "let's take a stroll" (see SANPO).

ASA 朝 morning

Asa begins at daybreak and ends at midmorning. This is in
contrast with English "morning," which begins earlier and
lasts longer. Eleven A.M. is still morning in English, but
Japanese *asa* does not normally refer to such late hours.
Eleven in the morning is *gozen juuichi-ji* "11 A.M." rather
than **asa no juuichi-ji* (lit., "11 in the morning").

⌈ ⌉
ASHI 足 **foot, leg**

In English, "foot" and "leg" are two different words, but in Japanese, *ashi* might mean either of them or both. *Ashi ga itai* may therefore mean "My leg hurts," "My legs hurt," "My foot hurts," "My feet hurt," or some combination thereof. It really doesn't matter since the person who feels the pain is likely to point to the painful spot anyway to indicate where he is hurting. Moreover, if it becomes necessary to be more specific (e.g., when one has to explain his ailment to his doctor over the phone), there are words for parts of legs and feet, e.g., *momo* "thigh," *hiza* "knee," *sune* "shin," *fukurahagi* "calf," *ashikubi* "ankle," *kakato* "heel," and so on.

⌈ ⌉
ASHITA あした **tomorrow**

The word for "tomorrow" is most often *ashita,* as in *Ashita wa ame ga furu ka mo shirenai* "It may rain tomorrow." In fact, that is the only word children use to mean "tomorrow." Adults, however, also use two synonyms for *ashita, asu,* and *myoonichi,* though not as frequently as *ashita. Asu* is more formal than *ashita,* and *myoonichi* is even more so. *Ashita* may appear in either informal or formal speech, while *asu* is more likely to appear in formal speech, and *myoonichi* is used only in very formal speech, as in *Mata myoonichi ojama-sasete-itadakimasu* "I shall pay you a visit again tomorrow."

Just as *ashita* has its formal counterparts, other temporal expressions have their formal counterparts. For example:

USUAL	FORMAL	
ototoi	*issakujitsu*	day before yesterday
kinoo	*sakujitsu*	yesterday

| *yuube* | *sakuban, sakuya* | last night |
| *asatte* | *myoogonichi* | day after tomorrow |

ASOBU 遊ぶ to play

The verb *asobu* means "to play."

(1) **Kodomo-tachi wa niwa de asonde-imasu.**

The children are playing in the yard.

Asobu, however, cannot be used in reference to sports, whether sports in general or specific sports such as *yakyuu* "baseball" or *tenisu* "tennis." Sports require *suru* "to do" instead. In (2) below, therefore, *shimashita* must be used.

(2) **Kinoo wa ichi-nichi-juu yakyuu o shimashita** (not *asobi-mashita).

Yesterday I played baseball all day.

Playing games also requires *suru.*

(3) **Toranpu o shimashoo** (not *asobimashoo).

Let's play cards.

(4) **Yuube wa ichi-ji made maa-jan o shimashita** (not *asobi-mashita).

Last night we played Mah Jongg until 1 o'clock.

Playing musical instruments requires different verbs, depending on the kind.

(5) **Piano o hiite-kudasai** (from **hiku**).

Please play the piano for me.

(6) **Toranpetto o fuite-iru** (from **fuku**) **no wa dare desu ka.**

Who is the person playing the trumpet?

Asobu sometimes means "to be idle, to be out of work, to be not in use."

(7) **Ano hito wa daigaku o sotsugyoo-shite kara, shuu-shoku-shinai de ichi-nen asonde-shimatta soo da.**

I hear he has idled away one whole year without getting a job since graduating from college.

(8) **Katta tochi o asobasete-oku no wa oshii desu yo.**
You shouldn't leave the piece of land you bought unused.

A very common idiom involving *asobu* is *asobi ni iku* (or *kuru*), meaning "to pay a social call."

(9) **Doozo ichi-do oasobi ni oide-kudasai.**
Please come and see us (*not* *come and play) some time.

ATAMA 頭 head

One puzzling expression for English speakers might be *atama o karu,* which literally means "to clip one's head," but actually is another version of *kami[noke] o karu* "to give someone a haircut, to get a haircut." We often use *atama o arau* (lit., "to wash one's head"), too, to mean *kami[noke] o arau* "to wash one's hair."

Two very common expressions containing *atama* are *atama ga ii* (lit., "the head is good") meaning "smart, bright, intelligent" and *atama ga warui* (lit., "the head is bad") meaning "stupid, dumb, dense."

(10) **Ano ko wa atama ga ii kara, nan de mo sugu oboeru.**
That child is so bright he learns everything quickly.

Atama and "head" do not necessarily refer to the same part of the human body. While "head" refers to that part of the body joined to the trunk by the neck, *atama* refers to that portion of the head roughly from the eyebrows up, plus the whole of the back of the head.

ATATAKAI 暖かゝい [pleasantly] warm

Atatakai (or, more colloquially, *attakai*) is almost always translated in English as "warm," but, unlike "warm," *atatakai* always carries a connotation of pleasantness. When we have a nice warm day in the midst of winter, or when winter gradually gives way to pleasant spring weather, we use *atatakai*. We do not use *atatakai*, but *atsui* "hot" instead, if, in the midst of summer, the mercury reaches, for example, the mid-80s Fahrenheit, although in English one often says "It's very *warm* today," on such a day.

Atatakai may be used with reference not only to weather but to liquids and solids as well. Study the following examples:

(1) **atatakai tenki (haru, hi,** etc.)—weather
    warm weather (spring, day, etc.)

(2) **atatakai nomimono (gyuunyuu, misoshiru,** etc.)—liquids
    warm beverage (milk, *miso* soup, etc.)

(3) **atatakai tabemono (te, gohan,** etc.)—solids
    warm food (hand, rice, etc.)

(See also ATSUI "hot" and NURUI "lukewarm.")

ATSUI 熱い, 暑い hot

In Japanese there are two words for "hot," both pronounced *atsui*. For the sake of convenience, I shall distinguish them here by calling one *atsui*$_1$ and the other *atsui*$_2$. They are represented by different *kanji* and are used with reference to different types of objects.

Atsui$_1$, written 熱い, is used in reference to gases, fluids, and solids.

(1) **atsui$_1$ kaze**
    a hot wind

(2) **atsui$_1$ ofuro**
    a hot bath

(3) **atsui₁ tabemono**
    hot food

Atsui₂, written 暑い, on the other hand, is used mainly in reference to weather, as in

(4) **Kyoo wa atsui₂.**
    It's hot today.

(5) **Ichiban atsui₂ tsuki wa shichi-gatsu ka hachi-gatsu da.**
    The hottest month is either July or August.

The difference between *atsui₁* when it is used in reference to gases, as in example (1) above, and *atsui₂* parallels the difference between *tsumetai* and *samui,* both of which mean "cold." *Atsui₁* refers to a sensation of heat affecting a limited part or parts of the body, such as the face and the hands, whereas *atsui₂* is used for a sensation of heat affecting the whole body. According to Kunihiro (p. 22), *atsui₁* belongs to one series of temperature words:

tsumetai, cold   *nurui,* lukewarm   *atatakai,* warm   *atsui₁*

while *atsui₂* is part of the other series:

samui, cold   *suzushii,* cool   *atatakai,* warm   *atsui₂*

(All these adjectives of temperature are explained in their respective entries.)

ATSUI 厚い **thick**

Atsui meaning "thick" requires a *kanji* different from the ones for *atsui* meaning "hot" (see ATSUI "hot"). This *atsui* is used in reference to flat objects.

(1) **atsui kami (hon, ita,** etc.)
    thick paper (book, board, etc.)

We also say *atsui oobaa* (lit., "a thick overcoat"), focusing on the thickness of the material, whereas the English speaker would speak of "a heavy overcoat" with the weight of the overcoat in mind.

Although, in English, "thick" may be used in reference to cylindrical objects as well as flat objects, as in "thick thread," "thick fingers," etc., that is not the case with *atsui*. *Futoi* is the correct adjective then.

(2) **futoi** (not *atsui) **ito** (**yubi, eda,** etc.)
    thick thread (fingers, branch, etc.)

Atsui "thick" has a different accent from *atsui* "hot." Whereas the latter is accented on the second syllable, the former is accentless. Thus examples (3) and (4), when spoken, may be differentiated only by accent.

(3) **atsui hottokeeki**
    thick pancakes

(4) **atsui hottokeeki**
    hot pancakes

AU 会う to see, to meet [someone]

In English, one says "see someone" or "meet someone," with "someone" as the direct object of "see" or "meet." In Japanese, on the other hand, *au* is an intransitive verb and takes the particle *ni* rather than *o*.

(1) **Tanaka-san wa mainichi gaarufurendo ni atte-iru rashii.**
    Mr. Tanaka seems to be seeing his girlfriend every day.

(2) **Yamashita-san ni hajimete atta no wa go-nen-gurai mae datta.**
    It was about five years ago that I met Mr. Yamashita for the first time.

Au can refer to seeing or meeting someone either by accident or on purpose. For example, in (3) below, *au* together with *pattari* "unexpectedly" refers to an accidental encounter (in this case, *au* is synonymous with *deau* "to meet by chance"), whereas in (4) *au* obviously signals meeting someone for some purpose.

(3) **Kinoo densha no naka de Yoshida-san ni pattari atta.**
Yesterday I met Mr. Yoshida on the train by chance.

(4) **Kyoo no gogo Satoo-san ni au yotei da.**
I plan to meet Mr. Sato this afternoon (e.g., to discuss some matter).

Seeing a doctor for medical reasons is not *au* but *mite-morau* "to have oneself seen."

(5) **Kubi ga itai kara, ashita isha ni mite-morau** (not *au) **tsumori desu.**
Because I have a neck-ache, I'm going to see my doctor tomorrow.

Meeting someone who is arriving at an airport, a station, etc., is not *au* but *mukae ni iku* "to go to welcome" or *mukae ni kuru* "to come to welcome."

(6) **Ato de chichi ga Narita ni tsuku no o mukae ni iku koto ni natte-iru.**
I am supposed to meet my father later when he arrives at Narita.

"Meet" sometimes means "to be introduced to." *Au* normally doesn't mean that. One must say something more specific to express that idea, as in

(7) **Kobayashi-san o goshookai-shimasu.**
I'd like you to meet Mr. Kobayashi. (lit., I'm going to introduce Mr. Kobayashi.)

Au corresponds to English "see [someone]" in the sense of "to meet up with and talk to" but usually not in the sense of "to catch sight of" or "to look at" (Jorden, 1, p. 171). For the latter, use *miru* "to look at" (see MIRU) or *mikakeru* "to catch sight of" instead.

BAN 晩 evening, night

Unlike *yoru* "night," *ban* is an anthropocentric term, i.e., a word closely tied to man's daily life. It roughly refers to the time span from dinner time until bedtime, and thus covers a slightly narrower range of time than does *yoru* (although there are some exceptions to this rule, most notably *hito-ban-juu* "all night long," which is synonymous with *yoru-juu*). Nine P.M., for example, could be called either *ban* or *yoru,* but 2 A.M. is more likely called *yoru* than *ban.* When one talks solely about the natural phenomenon of night with no reference to human life, *yoru* is the only choice (Tokugawa and Miyajima, pp. 409–10), as in

(1) **Tsuki wa yoru ga samui.**

Night on the moon is frigid.

BAN-GOHAN 晩ご飯, 晩御飯 evening meal

Although there are other variants meaning the same thing, *ban-gohan* is probably the most common word in speech for "evening meal." In America, the evening meal is the biggest meal and is called dinner, but dinner is not always served in the evening; on Sundays, for instance, some families serve dinner at lunchtime. In Japan, too, the evening meal is the main meal, but if, on some special occasion, the biggest meal of the day happens to be served at lunchtime, it has to be called *ohiru-gohan* "lunch" (lit., "noon meal"), and not *ban-gohan,* since *ban-gohan* literally means "evening meal." In other words, whereas dinner may be served at noon, in the afternoon, or in the evening, *ban-gohan* is always served in the evening, usually at 6 P.M. or thereabouts.

Other variants are *ban-meshi* (used by men only, informal

speech), *yuuhan* (used by both men and women; probably not as common as *ban-gohan*), and *yuushoku* (used in writing or in formal speech).

BENJO 便所 toilet

English has many expressions for "toilet," such as "bathroom," "washroom," "rest room," "men's room," "ladies' room," and "john." Likewise, Japanese has a variety of expressions for "toilet," of which *benjo* is one. The word should be avoided, however, in polite conversation. Use *tearai* (lit., "hand-washing [place]"), or *otearai* to be even more polite. *Toire,* derived from English "toilet," is also quite acceptable.

Using the word *benjo* is all right if used as part of compounds such as *suisen-benjo* "flush toilet" and *kooshuu-benjo* "public toilet."

BENKYOO 勉強 study

Benkyoo most often means "study."
(1) **Uchi no musuko wa ima juken-benkyoo-chuu desu.**
   Our son is in the midst of studying for entrance examinations.

The noun *benkyoo*, with the addition of the verb *suru* "to do," becomes the compound verb *benkyoo-suru* "to study."
(2) **Itsu Nihongo o benkyoo-shita n desu ka.**
   When did you study Japanese?

Having a learning experience is also *benkyoo*, especially in the expression *benkyoo ni naru.*

(3) **Sensei no ohanashi o ukagatte, taihen ii benkyoo ni narimashita.**

I learned a lot listening to your (lit., teacher's) talk. After hearing a talk, Americans commonly say to the speaker "I really enjoyed your talk." Japanese, on the other hand, would normally focus on what they learned from the talk, as in (3) above.

BOKU 僕 I, me

Boku meaning "I" is used only by males, and most often by boys and young men. Although young boys use *boku* on all occasions, adult men use it, or are supposed to use it, only on informal occasions. (On formal occasions, they normally switch to *watashi* or *watakushi.*)

The strangest use of *boku* occurs when, in some families, family members of a little boy who calls himself *boku* start calling him *boku* as well. This occurs, however, only when the little boy is the only, or the youngest, son in the family. *Boku* in this case is used, as it were, like the boy's given name. (In fact, the diminutive suffix -*chan,* which is normally attached to a child's name, as in *Yoshiko-chan,* is sometimes added to *boku,* forming *boku-chan.*)

(1) **Boku[-chan], hayaku irasshai.**

lit., Me, come here quickly.

This "fictive" use of *boku* is explained by Suzuki (p. 124) thus: "When she [i.e., a mother calling her son *boku*] speaks in this way, she is thinking of the boy as he would be called if viewed from the position of the youngest member of the family, in this case the boy himself. The boy would naturally call himself *boku.* Therefore, by identifying with him, adults in the family can call him *boku* as well."

BUKKA 物価 **prices**

Bukka means "general commodity prices."

(1) **Konogoro wa bukka ga takakute komarimasu nee.**

Isn't it terrible that prices are so high these days!

Bukka does not refer to the price of a specific object. For that, one has to use *nedan* "price" instead. In example (2), therefore, *nedan* must be used.

(2) **Gasorin no nedan** (not **bukka*) **ga mata agatta.**

The price of gasoline has gone up again.

BYOOKI 病気 **sick, sickness**

Byooki can be translated into English as either "sick" or "sickness," depending on the context.

(1) **Tanaka-san wa byooki desu.**

Mr. Tanaka is sick.

(2) **Gan wa iya na byooki da.**

Cancer is a nasty disease.

Unlike "sick," however, *byooki* cannot refer to a temporary state of being nauseous. To express that state, other expressions must be used.

(3) **Kuruma ni yotte-shimatta.**

I became carsick.

(4) **Chi o mite kimochi** (or **mune**) **ga waruku natta.**

I became sick at the sight of blood.

Unlike "sick," *byooki* does not refer to boredom or disgust. To express the idea of "I'm sick of parties," for example, one would have to say something like (5) or (6).

(5) **Paatii ga iya ni natta.**

lit., Parties have started boring me.

(6) **Paatii wa moo takusan da.**

lit., I can't take any more parties.

Whereas *genki* "healthy, well, vigorous," the opposite of *byooki,* is a *na*-noun, *byooki* is a genuine noun and therefore requires *no* instead of *na* when used in prenoun position. Note the difference between (7) and (8).

(7) **genki na** (not *genki no) **kodomo**
a healthy (*or* vigorous, lively) child

(8) **byooki no** (not *byooki na) **kodomo**
a sick child

CHICHI 父 father

When an adult talks to an outsider (i.e., a non-family member) about his own father, *chichi* is the correct term to be used.

(1) **Chichi wa moo hachijuu ni narimashita.**
My father has turned 80 already.

When an adult talks to a member of his family (e.g., his mother and siblings) about his father, he usually uses *otoo-san.* (Inside-the-family terms for *father* vary from family to family, e.g., *otoo-sama* and *papa,* but *otoo-san* is probably the most common.)

When an adult male is engaged in an informal conversation with close associates or friends, he is likely to refer to his father as *oyaji* "my old man." The use of *oyaji* is far more common in Japanese than that of "my old man" in English, but it is restricted to men only.

When an adult talks to an outsider about the latter's or someone else's father, *otoo-san* is probably the most common term.

The above rules apply to adults only. Children, whether boys or girls, most often use the term *otoo-san* in almost all situations.

CHIGAU 違う to be different, to be incorrect

Chigau has roughly two meanings: "to be different" and "to be incorrect."

(1) **Nihonjin wa Chuugokujin to zuibun chigau.**

The Japanese are quite different from the Chinese.

(2) **Kono kotae wa chigaimasu yo.**

This answer is incorrect, you know.

These two meanings may seem unrelated at first, but they are actually not as far apart as one may think. After all, an *incorrect* answer is an answer that is *different* from the correct one.

Iie, chigaimasu is often used in lieu of *Iie, soo ja arimasen* to mean "No, that's not so." *Iie* is frequently left out. The direct English translation of *Iie, chigaimasu* would be "No, it's incorrect"; English speakers might therefore feel that this Japanese expression is probably a strong denial. It is, however, not as strong as the English translation might suggest, and is at least as commonly used as *Iie, soo ja arimasen.*

As is the case with *Soo ja arimasen, Chigaimasu* is most often used to contradict a question ending with a noun + *desu ka.*

(3) A: **Are wa Tanaka-san desu ka.**

Is that Mr. Tanaka?

B: **Chigaimasu. Suzuki-san desu.**

No, that's Mr. Suzuki.

The use of *Chigaimasu* is not appropriate as a response to a question ending with an adjective + *desu ka,* or a verb + *ka* (see SOO DESU).

CHOOSEN 朝鮮 Korea

Most Japanese unfortunately have been rather prejudiced

against the Koreans for no apparent reason. Especially during the time when Korea was under Japanese rule (1910–45), the word *Choosenjin* "Korean[s]" was almost always uttered with contempt. It was for this reason that the name *Choosen* was almost completely discarded when Japan lost World War II. Since then the Japanese have adopted the names *Hokusen* for "North Korea" and *Kankoku* for "South Korea." What is really inconvenient, however, is the lack of an appropriate prejudice-free name for Korea as a whole. Linguists, for example, still have to refer to the Korean language as *Choosengo* since the language is one and the same in North Korea and in South Korea. The word *Kankokugo* (lit., "South Korean language"), which some people use, is not really an accurate label for the language.

CHOSHA 著者 the author

Chosha means "person who has written a specific (usually nonfiction) book."
(1) **Kono hon no chosha wa Tanaka Ichiroo to yuu hito desu.**
   The author of this book is called Ichiro Tanaka.

English "author" is broader in meaning. It can mean "person who has written a specific book" (as in "He is the author of this book") or "person who writes books" (as in "He is an author"). *Chosha* can never be used in the latter sense. (See also SAKKA and SHOOSETSUKA.)

CHOTTO ちょっと a little

Chotto is very much like *sukoshi*.
(1) **Kyoo wa chotto** (or **sukoshi**) **samui.**
   It's a bit cold today.

(2) **Onaka ga suite-inai kara, chotto** (or **sukoshi**) **shika taberarenakatta.**

Since I wasn't hungry, I could eat only a little.

The only difference between *chotto* and *sukoshi* in the above examples is that *chotto* is perhaps slightly more conversational than *sukoshi*.

Chotto, however, is used on many other occasions where *sukoshi* would be inappropriate. This occurs especially when one wishes to soften a request, as in (3) below, or express reluctance in a polite way, as in (4).

(3) **Chotto misete-kudasai.**

Would you please show it to me?

Chotto in this sentence does not mean "a little." Rather it expresses the idea that the request being made is not a significant one. It is almost like saying "May I ask a small favor?" The use of *chotto* in requests is very common; in fact, in stores and restaurants some customers use *Chotto!* by itself when they wish to catch the attention of a salesclerk or waitress.

(4) A : **Ashita kite-itadakemasu ka.**

Could you come tomorrow?

B : **Ashita wa chotto.**

I'm afraid I can't.

The answer in (4) literally means "Tomorrow is a little [inconvenient]." Japanese speakers don't normally reject requests, suggestions, and invitations flatly with *Iie* "No" since that would make them sound too direct and discourteous; they prefer to use *chotto,* which sounds less direct and more tactful.

DAIGAKU 大学 **college, university**

"College" and "university" are both *daigaku* in Japanese.

Although one can use *tanka-daigaku* (lit., "single-subject *daigaku*") for "college" and *soogoo-daigaku* (lit., "comprehensive *daigaku*") for "university," these terms are more or less for dictionaries only and are never attached to college or university names, nor are they much used in speech.

Most Japanese are unaware of the usage difference between "college" and "university" in the United States, and simplistically believe that "university" is a more prestigious term than "college." The official English translations of the names of Japanese colleges and universities are, consequently, always something like "The University of So-and-so." It is for this reason that the names of some Japanese institutions of higher learning sound very strange in English, e.g., "The X University of Science" or "The Y University of Economics."

DAIJOOBU 大丈夫 **all right**

Daijoobu is, to a certain extent, like "all right." For example, if you see someone fall, you run up to him and ask *Daijoobu desu ka* meaning "Are you all right?" But there are some situations where *daijoobu* cannot be used to mean "all right." For example, in English, if someone asks "How are you?" you might answer "All right," meaning "Fine." *Daijoobu* could not be used in a comparable situation in Japanese unless you happened to have been ill. In English, you can also say "All right!" when something turns out the way you were hoping it would, e.g., your favorite baseball team scores a run in a crucial inning. In Japanese, *Ii zo!* (lit., "Great!") would be used in that case instead of *daijoobu*. Likewise, *daijoobu* may not be used in accepting a suggestion. In English, if someone suggests "Let's go to a movie," you can indicate your willingness by answering "All right," but in Japanese you would have to say *Ee, ikimashoo* "Yes, let's go."

To summarize, *daijoobu* is most appropriate when there is a good reason for concern. The function of *daijoobu* is to dispel that concern. In other words, it is an expression of reassurance. Study the following examples:

(1) A: **Abunai!**

      Look out!

   B: **Daijoobu desu yo.**

      I'm all right.

(2) A: **Tanaka-san ni anna shigoto ga dekiru deshoo ka.**

      Do you think Mr. Tanaka can handle that kind of job?

   B: **Daijoobu desu yo.**

      He'll be all right.

In both examples above, *Daijoobu desu yo* can be paraphrased as "Although you may have a good reason to worry, you don't really have to."

DAKE だけ **only**

Although *dake* often corresponds to English "only," as in sentences (1) and (2) below, it does not carry a negative overtone, as "only" does.

(1) **Tanaka-san dake kite, hoka no hito wa konakatta.**

Only Mr. Tanaka came; nobody else did.

(2) Housewife (to maid): **Kaimono ni iku nara, gyuunyuu dake katte-kite-moraeba ii wa.**

If you're going shopping, the only thing I'd like you to buy is milk.

The positive overtone in *dake* becomes clear when *dake* is contrasted with *shika . . . nai,* which always carries a negative connotation.

(3) **Tanaka-san dake kita.**
Only Mr. Tanaka came. (i.e., Mr. Tanaka alone came.)
(4) **Tanaka-san shika konakatta.**
Only Mr. Tanaka came. (i.e., No one but Mr. Tanaka came.)

In (3), the speaker's focus is on the fact that Mr. Tanaka came (though he was the only one who came). On the other hand, in (4), the speaker's focus is on the fact that nobody else came. It is because of this difference between *dake* and *shika . . . nai* that we can use only *dake* in (5), and only *shika . . . nai* in (6).

(5) **Hoka no hito wa konakatta keredo, Tanaka-san**
| (a) **dake wa kita.** |
| (b) **shika konakatta.* |
Nobody else came, but Mr. Tanaka, though he was the only one, did come.

(6) **Okane ga ni-doru**
| (a) *dake atta |
| (b) **shika nakatta** | **kara, eiga e ikarenakatta.**
Since I had only (i.e., no more than) two dollars, I couldn't go to the movies.

DEKAKERU 出かける **to go out**

Dekakeru is usually translated into English as "to go out" and is therefore often confused by American students of Japanese with *deru,* which is also matched up with "to go out." *Dekakeru,* however, is quite different from *deru* in that it is used only in reference to human beings. For example, in sentence (1), either *dekakeru* or *deru* may be used, but in sentence (2), only *deru* would be correct.

(1) **Chichi wa kyoo dekakete-imasu** (or **dete-imasu**).
My father is out today.

(2) **Konban wa ku-ji-goro tsuki ga deru** (not *dekakeru*) **hazu da.**

The moon is expected to be out about nine tonight.

Dekakeru also differs from *deru* in that it specifically refers to leaving one's abode, whereas *deru* may refer to going out of any place. "To go out of a room" would therefore be *heya o deru* (not *dekakeru*).

Furthermore, *dekakeru* is different from *deru* in that it implies some sort of outing covering a distance, be it a walk, a visit, or a trip. *Deru,* on the other hand, is noncommital as to distance or reason. In sentence (7), therefore, only (a) is correct.

(7) **Tonari no denwa o kari ni** | (a) **uchi o deta.**
     | (b) *dekaketa.*

I left the house to ask the next-door neighbor to let me use the phone.

Dekakeru meaning "to go out" is accentless. This word should not be confused with *de-kakeru* "to be about to go out," which is accented. This latter is a compound verb formed by the *-te* form of *deru* followed by *kakeru* "to be about to do such-and-such," and is used as follows:

(8) **Tsuki ga de-kakete** (not *dekakete*) **mata kumo ni kakureta.**

The moon was about to come out but hid again behind the clouds.

DEKIRU できる, 出来る to come about, to be able to

Roughly speaking *dekiru* has two meanings: (a) "to come about, to be born, to be produced, to be built, to be completed," as in sentences (1) and (2) below, and (b) "to be possible, to be able to, can do," as in (3) and (4).

(1) **Suupu ga dekita.**
   The soup is ready. (lit., The soup has come about.)
(2) **Asoko ni atarashii depaato ga dekita.**
   A new department store has been built over there. (lit.,
   A new department store has come about over there.)
(3) **Watanabe-san wa eigo ga yoku dekiru.**
   Mr. Watanabe is very good in English. (lit., Mr. Watanabe can do English well.)
(4) **Ano hito wa gorufu ga dekiru.**
   He knows how to play golf. (lit., He can do golf.)
At first glance, these two meanings do not seem to have
much in common; but, on second thought, they are related,
for if you know how to do something, it does "come about"
for you.

Since the original meaning of *dekiru* is "to come about"
(Morita, p. 309), the subject marker *ga* rather than the object
marker *o* is used with it even when it means "can do."
(5) **Watanabe-san wa eigo ga** (not *o) **dekiru.**
   Mr. Watanabe is good in English.

Dekiru in the sense of "can do" is used much less often in
Japanese than "can" is in English. The reason is that in
Japanese many verbs have their own potential forms. For
example, *taberu* "to eat" has the potential form, *taberareru*
"can eat," and *yomu* "to read" has *yomeru* "can read."
Although it is also grammatically correct to say *taberu koto
ga dekiru* "one can eat" or *yomu koto ga dekiru* "one can
read," these forms are lengthier and are therefore not used
as often. In fact, *dekiru* is basically used only as the potential form of *suru* "to do." It cannot even be used in place of
the potential forms of other verbs. In English, it is perfectly correct to say "Yes, I can" in response to "Can you read
this?" for example. In Japanese, on the other hand, the
answer in (6) below would be incorrect.

(6) A: **Kore ga yomemasu ka.**
Can you read this?
B: **Hai,** *dekimasu.*
Yes, I can.

Dekimasu in this case must be replaced by *yomemasu,* the same potential verb meaning "can read" that appears in the question.

DENSHA 電車 [electric] train

Densha literally means "electric train," but oddly enough, not all electric trains are called *densha.* Long-distance trains run by the Japan National Railways used to be pulled by steam engines and were called *kisha* (lit., "steam trains"). Although these steam engines have long since been replaced by electric ones, trains that serve the same lines are even now called *kisha* by force of habit.

DENWA 電話 telephone

Denwa is a noun meaning "telephone."

(1) **Kono hen ni denwa wa arimasen ka.**
Is there a telephone around here?

One difference between *denwa* and "telephone" is that *denwa* is often used to mean "telephone call" whereas "telephone" is not.

(2) **Kinoo Tanaka-san kara denwa ga arimashita.**
There was a telephone call (lit., There was a telephone) from Mr. Tanaka yesterday.

In English, "telephone" is also used as a verb; in Japanese, on the other hand, *suru* has to be added to change *denwa* into a verb, that is, *denwa-suru* "to telephone [someone]."

(3) **Yoshida-san ni denwa-shite kudasai.**
    Please call Mr. Yoshida.

Denwa o kakeru "to make a phone call" and *denwa o ireru,* a fairly new coinage meaning "to give [someone] a call," may also be used in place of *denwa-suru,* as in

(4) **Yoshida-san ni denwa o kakete** (or **irete**) **kudasai.**
    Please give Mr. Yoshida a call.

When the person to whom the phone call is made is not mentioned or even implied, only *denwa o kakeru* is acceptable. In (5), therefore, only (a) would be correct.

(5) **Uchi no ko wa**
    (a) **denwa o kakeru** | **no ga suki de komarimasu.**
    (b) **denwa o ireru*
    (c) **denwa-suru*

Our child likes making phone calls too much.

DERU 出る to go out, to leave, to graduate

Deru most often means "to go out, to come out, to get out."

(1) **Amari atsui kara, niwa ni demashoo.**
    It's so hot; let's go out into the yard.

(2) **Nihon o deta no wa nijuu-nen mae datta.**
    It was 20 years ago that I left Japan.

With reference to school, *deru* is used as a synonym for *sotsugyoo-suru* "to graduate."

(3) **Daigaku o dete** (or **sotsugyoo-shite**) **kara nani o suru tsumori desu ka.**
    What do you plan to do after graduating from college?

Don't equate *deru* meaning "to graduate" with English "get out" since "to get out of school" might mean "to leave school without graduating."

This latter meaning would be expressed in Japanese by another verb: *chuutai-suru* "to drop out of school."
(4) **Ano hito wa daigaku o chuutai-shite haiyuu ni natta soo desu.**

I hear he dropped out of college and became an actor. (See also DEKAKERU.)

DONNA どんな **what kind [of]**

Whereas, in English, "what kind" can be used alone without "of" + noun, Japanese *donna* has to be followed by a noun.
(1) **Kore wa donna shoosetsu desu ka.**

What kind of novel is this?

In questions like this, *dooyuu* can also be used to mean "what kind."
(2) **Kore wa dooyuu shoosetsu desu ka.**

(same meaning as 1 above)

When *donna* and *dooyuu* are used in *te mo* (or *de mo*) clauses meaning "no matter . . . ," however, there is a difference between the two (Tokugawa and Miyajima, p. 294). *Dooyuu* in such clauses can signal only "[no matter] what kind," whereas *donna* can be used to mean either "[no matter] what kind" or "[no matter] to what degree." Compare the following:
(3) **Donna (or Dooyuu) koto ni natte mo kamaimasen.**

I don't care what happens. (lit., No matter what kind of result ensues, I don't care.)
(4) **Donna (not *Dooyuu) samui toki de mo jogingu o shimasu.**

I jog no matter how cold it is.

In (3), either *donna* or *dooyuu* may be used because "what kind" is the issue; in (4), however, only *donna* is correct because *dooyuu* cannot mean "how" in the sense of "to what degree."

DŌO ITASHIMASHITE どう致しまして Not at all, You are welcome

Doo itashimashite, with or without a preceding *Iie,* serves as a response to someone's expression of gratitude. In (1) below, therefore, all of speaker B's answers are correct.

(1) A: **Doomo arigatoo gozaimashita.**
      Thank you very much for what you did for me.
   B: (a) **Iie.**
      (b) **Doo itashimashite.**
      (c) **Iie, doo itashimashite.**
         Not at all.

It is safer not to equate *Doo itashimashite* with English "You are welcome," because *Doo itashimashite* may also be used as a response to apologies.

(2) A: **Doomo gomeiwaku o okake-shimashita.**
      I'm very sorry for causing so much trouble.
   B: **Doo itashimashite.**
      Not at all.

In some cases, *Doo itashimashite* may also be used in response to compliments (Jorden, 1, p. 3), but that particular use is very limited. It is much safer, therefore, to say just *Iie,* which is always a correct response to compliments. (See also ARIGATOO GOZAIMASU and IIE.)

DŌOMO どうも Thanks, Sorry

Doomo is most often an abbreviation of *Doomo arigatoo*

gozaimasu (or *gozaimashita*) "Thank you very much" or *Doomo shitsurei-shimashita* "I am very sorry for what I have done." Lately, *Doomo* seems to have started developing a wider and wider range of meaning, however. Thus it is beginning to function as a salutation in a tremendous number of situations. Some people use it in lieu of other more established greetings such as *Konnichi wa* "Good day!" and *Sayonara* "Good-by!" and, according to Maruya (p. 153), even *Moshimoshi* (a greeting on the phone, meaning "Hello!"). Its usage has become so broad that Maruya suggests (p. 154), though tongue in cheek, that it may someday even acquire the meaning of "I love you"!

⌐DOOZO どうぞ please

Doozo by itself is most often used when one invites someone to do something, e.g., when a host or a hostess invites a guest to come in, or when one offers someone something such as food, a beverage, or a cigarette. (Offering something to someone is really like inviting that person to have and enjoy the item offered.)

Doozo by itself rarely functions as a request. It may, however, be attached to a request.

(1) **Doozo onegai-shimasu.**
    Please do me this favor.
(2) **Doozo okamai naku.**
    Please don't bother.

English-speaking students of Japanese often make the error of assuming that *doozo* makes requests more polite, as does "please" in English. Adding *doozo* to a request, does not make it any more polite—it just intensifies it. For example, in (1) above, the politeness lies not in the word *doozo,* but in the verb *onegai-shimasu* (lit., "I humbly request"), which is the polite-humble form of *negau* "to request." In fact, Japanese polite requests are uttered more often without *doozo* than English polite requests are made without "please."

⌐ E 絵 picture

E means "picture," but only in reference to a drawn or painted picture. Unlike English "picture" it cannot refer to a movie or a photograph. A movie is an *eiga,* and a photograph is a *shashin. E* may mean "photograph" only in the compound *e-hagaki* "picture postcard."

⌐ EE ええ yes

Ee is a more conversational version of *hai.* Use it, however, only as a response to a question.
(1) A: **Are wa Ueda-san deshoo ka.**
       Might that be Mr. Ueda?
    B: **Ee, soo desu yo.**
       Yes, it is.
Do not use *ee* as a response to a knock on the door or the calling of your name. For that purpose, only *hai* is appropriate.

EIGA 映画 movie

English has many words meaning "motion picture"; Japanese has only one, *eiga.* Although "movie" means both "motion picture" and "movie theater," *eiga* means only "motion picture." A movie theater is *eigakan*. "To go to a movie" is *eiga e* (or *ni*) *iku,* but not *eigakan e (or *ni*) *iku.*

Until the 1930s or so, movies were called *katsudoo-shashin* (or *katsudoo* for short), which literally means "motion picture." It was a very common word until it was gradually replaced by *eiga,* which is now the only term for "movie."

ENPITSU 鉛筆 pencil

In English, not only a regular pencil but also a mechanical pencil may be called a pencil. In Japanese, however, *enpitsu* refers to a regular pencil only. A mechanical pencil is called *shaapu-penshiru,* or simply *shaapu,* which is traceable to "Eversharp," the brand name of the first U.S.-made mechanical pencil.

FURUI 古い old

Furui meaning "old" is used, as a rule, in reference to inanimate things.

(1) **Anna furui uchi wa kawanai hoo ga ii desu yo.**
    You shouldn't buy an old house like that.
(2) **Kono oobaa mo zuibun furuku natta.**
    This overcoat has gotten quite old.

With reference to persons, other words such as *toshi o totta* "old, aged," *toshiyori* "old person," and *roojin* "old person" have to be used.

(3) **Murata-san mo toshi o totta nee.**
    Hasn't Mr. Murata grown old!
(4) **Asoko ni toshiyori no obaasan ga suwatte-iru deshoo.**

Do you see that old lady sitting over there?

(5) **Ano roojin-tachi ni seki o yuzuroo.**

Let's give our seats to those old people.

When *furui* is used with reference to persons, it can carry different meanings.

(6) **Kono kaisha de ichiban furui no wa Yamada-san da.**

The person with the most seniority in this firm is Mr. Yamada.

(7) **Ano hito wa moo furui.**

He is passé (*or* behind the times)

Furui is sometimes shortened to *furu* and added to other words to form compounds.

(8) **furu-hon, furu-gi, furu-shinbun**

used books, used clothes, old newspapers

GAIJIN 外人 foreigner

Gaijin, in a broad sense, means "foreigner." In a narrower sense, however, it refers only to Caucasians, especially those staying in Japan.

Gaikokujin (lit., "foreign-country person"), another word for "foreigner," on the other hand, is more general and simply means "alien (from any country and of any color)."

GAKKOO 学校 school

In English, "school" not only refers to nursery school through high school, but sometimes may refer to a college, university, or part thereof, as in

(1) Harvard is a famous school.

(2) That university has a law school, a medical school, an engineering school, etc.

Gakkoo, on the other hand, normally refers to schools from the elementary-school level through the high-school level only. Sentence (1) and (2) above, therefore, would be translated into Japanese without the use of *gakkoo.*

(3) **Haabaado wa yuumei na daigaku** (not *gakkoo) **desu.**
    Harvard is a famous university.
(4) **Ano daigaku ni wa hoo-gakubu, i-gakubu, koo-gabuku** (not **hoo-gakkoo,* **i-gakkoo,* *koo-gakkoo) **nado ga arimasu.**
    That university has a law school, a medical school, an engineering school, etc.

GAKUSEI 学生 student

Students in a formal educational system, i.e., nursery school through college, are called *seito* or *gakusei,* depending on the level. *Gakusei* refers to older students, especially college students. Students of high-school age or younger are usually referred to as *seito,* although high school students may sometimes be called *gakusei* also (see SEITO).

GEKIJOO 劇場 theater

Gekijoo means "theater" in the sense of "building or place where there is regularly a theatrical performance on the stage." Although some movie theaters may have names such as *X-gekijoo,* they are not *gekijoo* in the real sense of the word. Movie theaters are normally referred to as *eigakan* instead.

Unlike English "theater," *gekijoo* can never mean "drama" or "theater arts." (See also SHIBAI.)

GENKI 元気 healthy, well, high-spirited

Genki is most often used as the opposite of *byooki* "sick."
(1) **Nagai aida byooki deshita ga, moo genki ni narimashita.**
I was sick for a long time, but I'm fine now.
Genki may also refer to vigor or one's spirits.
(2) **Yamada-san wa okusan o nakushite genki ga nakatta ga, konogoro mata genki ni natte-kita.**
Mr. Yamada was in low spirits after he lost his wife, but lately he's been cheerful (*or* in better spirits) again.
(See also BYOOKI and OGENKI DESU KA.)

GOGO 午後 afternoon, P.M.

Gogo means "afternoon," as in
(1) **Ashita no gogo mata kite-kudasai.**
Please come again tomorrow afternoon.
Gogo also means "P.M.," but unlike "P.M.," which follows the time (i.e., "2 P.M.," "3 P.M.," etc.), it precedes the time.
(2) **gogo ni-ji**
2 P.M.
(See also GOZEN.)

GOHAN ご飯, 御飯 cooked rice, meal

In a narrow sense, *gohan* means "cooked rice."
(1) **Gohan o moo ip-pai kudasai.**
Please give me one more bowl of rice.
In a broader sense, *gohan* means "meal."
(2) **Moo sorosoro ohiru da kara, gohan ni shimashoo.**
Since it's almost noon, let's have lunch.
The fact that the same word may mean both "cooked

rice" and "meal" points to the important role cooked rice used to play in the traditional Japanese meal. The names of the three daily meals are, most commonly, *asa-gohan* "breakfast," *hiru-*(or *ohiru-*) *gohan* "lunch," and *ban-gohan* "dinner."

Men sometimes use the word *meshi* instead of *gohan*, especially in informal situations. *Meshi*, like *gohan*, means both "cooked rice" and "meal." There is another word meaning "cooked rice," i.e., *raisu* from English "rice." This word, however, has a very limited range of meaning, referring only to cooked rice served on a plate in a Western-style restaurant (Miura, p. 128). It never means "meal."

GOKUROO-SAMA ご苦労様 Thank you for your work

Gokuroo-sama is an expression of thanks for service rendered such as delivering things or running an errand, and "is most often said to newspaper boys, porters, bellboys, delivery men and the like . . . as a verbal tip" (Mizutani and Mizutani, 1, p. 117). It should not be used when someone "has done something for you out of sheer kindness" (ibid.), or when someone does something for his own good (e.g., someone who is studying hard for an examination or jogging for his own health and pleasure).

This greeting may sometimes be directed to a person of higher status. Since it is difficult to predict its appropriateness in a given situation, however, it might be safer to avoid the expression when addressing a person of higher status.

GOMEN-KUDASAI ごめんください Is anybody home?

When visiting a Japanese home, you first ring the bell and

wait for someone to answer. But what should you do if the bell is not working or if there is no bell at the front door? In that case, the best thing would be to shout out *Gomen-kudasai!* which literally means "Please excuse me" but is used in the sense of "Is anybody home?" If the door is not locked, you can even open the door (this is accepted behavior in Japan though totally unacceptable in the U.S.A.) and shout out *Gomen-kudasai!* (Cf. GOMEN-NASAI.)

GOMEN-NASAI ごめんなさい Sorry!

Gomen-nasai "Sorry!" is an apology used mostly at home between family members, especially by children apologizing to parents (Mizutani and Mizutani, pp. 14–15). Outside the home, too, *Gomen-nasai* is used mostly by children. An adult may say it, in informal situations, to someone lower in status. In formal situations, adults use *Shitsurei-shimasu* or *Shitsurei-shimashita* (see SHITSUREI-SHIMASU).

-GORO ごろ about, approximately

-Goro is a variant of *koro* "about, approximately" and is used exclusively as a suffix attached to nouns indicating points in time.

(1) **go-ji-goro**
   about 5 o'clock
(2) **san-gatsu-goro**
   about March

Because of the Japanese speaker's reluctance to be precise or exact, *-goro* is used more frequently in Japanese than "about" is used in English in reference to points of time. For example, instead of using *Nan-ji desu ka* to mean "What time is it?" many Japanese speakers ask *Nanji-goro desu ka* "About what time is it?" In English, however, "About what time is it?" is much rarer than "What time is it?"

Some speakers use *koro* instead of *-goro* to mean the same thing.

(3) **san-gatsu koro**
     about March

When not preceded by a noun, *koro,* not *-goro,* is the correct word. In the following sentence, therefore, *-goro* cannot be used.

(4) **Wakai koro** (not *-*goro) **wa yokatta!**
     Ah, those good old days when I was still young!

(See also KONOGORO and KORO.)

GOZEN 午前 A.M.

Gozen is the opposite of *gogo* meaning "P.M." (see GOGO).

(1) **Gozen san-ji desu ka, gogo san-ji desu ka.**
     Do you mean 3 A.M. or 3 P.M.?

Whereas *gogo* is often used adverbially, *gozen* is not. For example, while sentence (2) below is perfectly normal, (3) is a little unnatural.

(2) **Ashita no gogo kite-kudasai.**
     Please come tomorrow afternoon.

(3) *?Ashita no gozen kite-kudasai.*
     Please come tomorrow morning.

When used adverbially *gozen* usually takes the suffix *-chuu* "during."

(4) **Ashita no gozen-chuu kite-kudasai.**
     Please come tomorrow morning.

Sentence (4) is not synonymous with *Ashita no asa kite-*

kudasai since *gozen-chuu* covers a longer time span (i.e., up to noon) than *asa* does (see ASA).

⌐ -GURAI 〈ˇらい **about, approximately**

-Gurai, as well as its variant *-kurai,* indicates an approximate amount of anything.

(1) **Ano hon wa ikura ka shirimasen ga, tabun nisen-en-gurai deshoo.**
I'm not sure how much that book is, but it's probably about two thousand yen.

(2) **Ano hito wa gojuu-gurai deshoo.**
He is probably about fifty.

Although *-gurai* is quite similar in meaning to its English counterparts such as "about" and "approximately," it is probably used more often in Japanese than "about" or "approximately" are in English because of the Japanese speaker's reluctance to be too precise, definite, or specific. Japanese speakers often say to a salesclerk *Mittsu-gurai kudasai* (lit., "Give me about three"), for example, even when they want exactly three of something. This is the same psychology that leads them to say *nan-ji-goro* "about what time" instead of *nan-ji* "what time."

-Gurai is different from *-goro* (see -GORO) in that the latter is specifically for *points* in time (e.g., *san-ji-goro* "about 3 o'clock" and *roku-gatsu-goro* "about June") while the former is for *amounts* of anything. Some native speakers of Japanese do occasionally use *-gurai* with a word indicating a point in time, e.g., *ni-ji-gurai* instead of *ni-ji-goro* for "about 2 o'clock." This particular use of *-gurai,* however, is not really advisable.

HADAKA 裸 naked

To be described as *hadaka,* one does not have to be completely naked. A Japanese fisherman with nothing but a loincloth on may be described as *hadaka.* If a boy is lying down with nothing covering his upper body, his mother might say *Hadaka de nete-iru to kaze o hikimasu yo* "You'll catch a cold if you lie down half-naked." In a pickup basketball game in America, if one of the teams is shirtless, its members are called "the Skins." Their Japanese counterparts would be referred to as "*Hadaka.*"

To convey the meaning "completely naked," one would have to say *mappadaka* (lit., "truly naked").

HAHA 母 mother

Words for "mother" function in parallel to those for "father." The basic rules are: *haha* corresponds to *chichi, okaa-san* to *otoo-san,* and *ofukuro* to *oyaji* (see CHICHI).

HAI はい yes

Hai is used in response to questions (also requests, demands, and suggestions) to signal agreement or assent. Although *hai* is often equated with "yes," it is not the same as "yes"; it is more like "That's right." In fact, it corresponds to "yes" only when used as a response to affirmative questions. In response to negative questions, it corresponds to "no."

(1) A: **Wakarimasu ka.** (affirmative question)
    Do you understand?
   B: **Hai, wakarimasu.**
    Yes, I do. (lit., That's right. I understand.)

(2) A : **Wakarimasen ka.** (negative question)

Don't you understand?

B : **Hai, wakarimasen.**

No, I don't. (lit., That's right. I don't understand.)
From the above examples, the following becomes clear.
In English, what determines the choice between "yes" and
"no" is what follows; i.e., if what follows is in the affirmative (e.g., "I do"), you use "yes," whereas if what follows is
in the negative (e.g., "I don't"), you use "no." In Japanese,
on the other hand, what determines the choice of *hai* or *iie*
(see IIE) is whether you wish to indicate agreement or disagreement with the question. If you agree, you use *hai*, and
if you disagree, you use *iie;* whether what follows is in the
affirmative (e.g., *wakarimasu*) or in the negative (e.g.,
wakarimasen) is immaterial.

Hai, when used in response to negative questions, usually
corresponds to "no," as explained above. There are some
cases, however, where *hai* used as a response to negative
questions corresponds to "yes" instead.

(3) A : **Genki-soo ni natta ja arimasen ka.**

Aren't you looking perfectly well!

B : **Hai, okage-sama de kono goro wa sukkari genki ni
narimashita.**

Yes, I'm perfectly well now, thank you.
The above question, though negative in form, is actually
affirmative in spirit. What the question really means is
"You're looking perfectly well, and that's great!" Speaker B
therefore says *hai* to show agreement with the spirit of the
question. Consider two more examples.

(4) A : **Ashita mo kite-kuremasen ka.**

Will you come again tomorrow? (lit., Won't you
come again tomorrow?)

B : **Hai, ukagaimasu.**

Yes, I'll be glad to.

(5) A: **Tenki ga ii kara, yakyuu de mo shimasen ka.**

Since the weather is so nice, how about playing baseball or something (lit., shall we not play baseball or something)?

B: **Hai** (or **Ee**), **shimashoo.**

Yes, let's!

Although the A sentences above are negative in form, (4A) is actually a request with the meaning of "Please come again tomorrow," and (5A) is a suggestion meaning "How about doing such-and-such?" This use of *hai* is, therefore, not really an exception; it still follows the basic rule: If you are in agreement, use *hai*.

Hai is a formal expression. In less formal speech, *hai* is often replaced by *ee*. In even more informal speech (especially by men, youngsters, and little children), *un,* or simply *n,* is used.

In addition to the main use explained above, *hai* has other functions, some of which are described below. With the exception of (6), neither *ee* nor *un* can be used in place of *hai* in these examples.

Hai sometimes indicates "I'm listening" instead of "That's right."

(6) Boss: **Kinoo hanami ni ittara ne.**

Yesterday we went to see the cherry blossoms.

Employee: **Hai.**

Yes?

Boss: **Yuki ga futte-ki-chatta n da yo.**

It started snowing, of all things.

Hai, when used in response to the calling of one's name, signals "Here!" or "Present!" In (7) below, a teacher is taking attendance in class.

(7) Teacher: **Tanaka-san.**

Miss Tanaka!

Miss Tanaka: **Hai.**
Here!

Hai serves to draw the addressee's attention, for example, when one hands something to someone (e.g., when a sales-clerk gives change back to a customer), as in (8), or when a student raises his hand to draw the teacher's attention, as in sentence (9).

(8) Salesclerk: **Hai. Go-hyaku-en no otsuri desu.**
Here you are. Five hundred yen.

(9) Student: **Hai!** (raising his hand)
Sir?
Teacher: **Nan desu ka.**
What is it?
Student: **Chotto shitsumon ga aru n desu ga.**
May I ask you a question?

HAKU はく **to put on, to wear**

Haku is reserved for wearing hosiery (e.g., *kutsushita* "socks" and *sutokkingu* "stockings"), footwear (e.g., *kutsu* "shoes" and *buutsu* "boots"), and other items that are worn on the lower part of the body by putting one's legs through them (e.g., *sukaato* "skirt" and *zubon* "trousers").

(1) **Nihon no josei wa itsu-goro kara sukaato o haku yoo ni natta n deshoo ka.**
I wonder when Japanese women started wearing skirts.

(2) **Kono-goro no onna-no-hito wa tenki ga yokute mo buutsu o haite-iru.**
Women these days wear boots even when the weather is good.

As a rule, the act of putting on certain items is *haku* while the state of wearing them is *haite-iru*. In (3), for example, where the act of putting shoes on is the issue, only *haku* can be used whereas in (4) where the state of wearing a skirt is the issue, *haite-iru* is correct.

(3) **Nihonjin wa uchi o deru mae ni kutsu o haku** (not *haite-iru).

Japanese put on their shoes before leaving the house.

(4) **Asoko ni pinku no sukaato o haite-iru** (not *haku) **onna-no-hito ga iru deshoo.**

Do you see that woman who is wearing a pink skirt?

(See also HAMERU, KABURU, and KIRU.)

HAMERU はめる **to put on, to wear**

Things that one puts on by putting a hand or fingers through them require the verb *hameru*.

(1) **yubiwa (udewa, udedokei, tebukuro, guroobu,** etc.) **o hameru**

to put on a ring (a bracelet, a wristwatch, gloves, a baseball glove, etc.)

Hameru is often replaced by *suru*.

(2) **Samui hi ni wa tebukuro o hameta** (or **shita**) **hoo ga ii.**

It's better to wear gloves on cold days.

HATARAKU 働く **to work**

Hataraku means "to work" as in

(1) **Tonari no otetsudai-san wa itsumo daidokoro de hata-raite-iru.**

The maid next door is always working in the kitchen.

(2) **Ano kooba no kooin-tachi wa yoku hataraku.**

The workers at that factory work very hard.

Although *hataraku* and *shigoto o suru* "to do a job" are

similar in meaning, the latter is probably more appropriate for desk work.

(3) **Ano sakka wa hiruma ni nete, yoru shigoto o suru soo da.**
I hear that novelist sleeps during the day and works at night.

English "work" is sometimes almost synonymous with "study," e.g.,

(4) He is working for his doctorate.

In Japanese, however, *hataraku* cannot be used in that sense. Studying is referred to as *benkyoo-suru* (see BENKYOO).

(5) **Kare wa hakushigoo o toru tame ni benkyoo-shite-iru.**
He is studying for a doctorate.

Unlike "work," *hataraku* cannot be used in reference to pastimes and hobbies. Therefore, to express the idea of "work" as expressed in (6) below, some word other than *hataraku* would have to be used, as in (7).

(6) He is working hard to organize his stamp collection in his spare time.

(7) **Kare wa hima na toki kitte no korekushon o isshooken-mei seiri-shite-iru.**
lit., He is assiduously organizing his stamp collection in his spare time.

In English, if you are an employee of General Motors, you "work for" General Motors. *Hataraku* cannot be used in this sense. *Tsutomete-iru* (see TSUTOMERU) is the correct word.

(8) **Kare wa Sonii ni tsutomete-iru.**
He works for Sony. (lit., He is employed at Sony.)

HAYAI 速い fast; 早い early

Hayai means both "fast," as in sentence (1), and "early," as in (2).

(1) **Jidoosha wa jitensha yori hayai.**

Automobiles are faster than bicycles.

(2) **Hayakawa-san wa okiru no ga hayai.**

Mr. Hayakawa gets up early.

These two meanings of *hayai,* however, require two different *kanji.* In the sense of "fast, quick, speedy," *hayai* is usually written 速い, while in the sense of "early," it is always written 早い.

Although context usually makes the meaning quite clear, the word could be ambiguous in some cases, as in

(3) **hayai basu**

a fast (*or* early) bus

This ambiguity can be avoided, however, by the use of other expressions.

(4) **supiido ga hayai basu**

a fast bus (lit., a bus whose speed is fast)

(5) **asa hayai basu**

an early morning bus

HAZUKASHII 恥ずかしい **ashamed, shameful, shy, embarrassed, embarrassing**

The Japanese sense of morality is shame oriented while the Western counterpart is sin oriented, so say a number of scholars including Ruth Benedict, author of *The Chrysanthemum and the Sword.* It is probably true. Japanese speakers certainly use the word *hazukashii* very frequently.

(1) **Musuko ga hen na koto o shite hazukashii.**

I am ashamed that my son behaved so strangely.

(2) **Aitsu wa hazukashii yatsu da.**

He is a shameful scoundrel.

(3) **Ano ko wa hazukashii rashikute koko e ki-tagaranai.**

That child apparently feels shy; he doesn't want to come out here.

"Ashamed" and "shy" are two entirely different adjectives in English, but in Japanese *hazukashii* takes care of both. Obviously, in the Japanese speaker's mind, being ashamed and being shy have something in common. A person who feels ashamed does not wish to face others. The same holds true with a shy person.

HENJI 返事 answer

Henji is a noun meaning "answer, reply." Most often it refers to the act of saying *Hai* when one's name is called, as in sentence (1), or the act of writing a reply to a letter, as in (2).

(1) **"Tanaka-san!" to yonda no ni henji ga nakatta.**
I called out, "Mr. Tanaka!" but there was no answer.

(2) **Tegami o morattara sugu henji o dasu koto ni shite-iru.**
I make it a rule to write a reply as soon as I receive a letter.

In sentence (1) above, *henji* is synonymous with *kotae,* which also means "answer," but in sentence (2), *henji* cannot be replaced by *kotae.*

As a variation of sentence (1) above, *henji* might refer to the act of responding to a knock on the door or to a doorbell by saying *Hai!*

(3) **Nokku o shitara** (or **Yobirin o narashitara**) **"Hai!" to henji ga atta.**
When I knocked on the door (*or* rang the doorbell), someone answered, "Coming!"

Henji cannot be used to mean "answering the telephone." The verb *deru* would have to be used.

(4) **Denwa ga natte-iru no ni, dare mo denakatta** (not *henji o shinakatta*).
Although the phone was ringing, nobody answered.

HI 日 day, sun

Hi means "day," as in
(1) **Sono hi wa samukatta.**
It was cold that day.
(2) **Haru ni wa hi ga nagaku naru.**
The days become longer in the spring.
Hi also means "sun."
(3) **Ashita wa nanji-goro hi ga noboru daroo.**
I wonder what time the sun will rise tomorrow.
(4) **Kono heya wa hi ga yoku ataru kara attakai.**
This room is warm because it's very sunny (lit., because it's well exposed to the sun).

There is another word meaning "sun," *taiyoo*. There is, however, a definite difference between *hi* meaning "sun" and *taiyoo* in that the latter refers to the sun as the central body of the solar system, while *hi* is conceived of as a heavenly body that, like *tsuki* "moon," rises and sets around us humans. In other words, *hi* is an anthropocentric term while *taiyoo* is scientific, objective, and detached. Therefore, when one talks about sunspots, the solar system, solar observation, the diameter of the sun, etc., *taiyoo* rather than *hi* has to be used.
(5) **taiyoo** (not *hi*) **no kokuten**
sunspots
(6) **taiyoo** (not *hi*) **no chokkei**
the diameter of the sun

Hi is accentless when it is used in the sense of "sun," but it becomes accented when it is used in the sense of "day" and has a modifier, as in (1) and (7).

(7) **Samui ⌈hi⌉ni wa dare mo kimasen deshita.**
On cold days nobody came.

HIKUI 低い **low**

Hikui "low" is the opposite of *takai* meaning "high" (not *takai* meaning "expensive").

(1) **hikui yama (tana, kumo,** etc.)
low mountain (shelf, cloud, etc.)

Hikui corresponds to English "short" when a person's height is the issue.

(2) **se ga hikui hito**
short person (lit., person whose height is low)

In this case, however, *hikui* has to be preceded by *se ga,* and cannot by itself mean "short."

The opposite of *takai* meaning "expensive" is not *hikui* but *yasui* "cheap, inexpensive" (see YASUI). However, *hikui* as well as *yasui* may be used in connection with nouns such as *nedan* "price," *bukka* "commodity prices," and *chingin* "wage."

(3) **hikui** (or **yasui**) **nedan (bukka, chingin,** etc.)
low (*or* cheap) price (commodity prices, wage, etc.)

HIROI 広い **wide, broad, spacious**

Hiroi can be either one-dimensional as in (1) or two-dimensional as in (2).

(1) **hiroi michi (katahaba, rooka,** etc.)
   wide road (shoulders, corridor, etc.)
(2) **hiroi heya (niwa, kuni,** etc.)
   spacious room (yard, country, etc.)

When used two-dimensionally, *hiroi* is similar in meaning to *ookii* "large." But while *ookii* refers objectively to large size, *hiroi* implies subjective awareness of spaciousness for a particular purpose. As Morita states (p. 260), even an *ookii torikago* "large birdcage" isn't *hiroi* "spacious" if an ostrich is placed in it. (See also SEMAI, the opposite of *hiroi*.)

HIRU 昼 noon, daytime

Hiru has two basic meanings: "noon" and "daytime." In the following examples *hiru* means "noon" in (1), and "daytime" in (2).
(1) **Doyoo wa hiru made kurasu ga aru.**
   On Saturdays, there are classes until noon.
(2) **Hiru wa atsui ga, yoru wa suzushiku naru.**
   In the daytime it is hot, but at night it gets cooler.

Hiru is sometimes used as an abbreviation of *hiru-gohan* "lunch" (lit., "noon meal"), as in
(3) **Moo hiru[-gohan] wa tabemashita ka.**
   Have you had lunch yet?

For some strange reason, the honorific prefix *o-* may precede *hiru* in the sense of "noon" but not *hiru* meaning "daytime." *Ohiru* therefore can mean only "noon," but not "daytime." *Hiru* in the sense of "daytime" may be construed to be an abbreviation of *hiruma* "daytime," which never takes the prefix *o-* either. *Hiruma*, unlike *hiru*, can never mean "noon."

HITO 人 person

Hito means "person."
(1) **Kimura-san wa ii hito desu ne.**
    Mr. Kimura is a nice person, isn't he!

In very polite speech, use *kata* instead of *hito* when talking about someone to whom you wish to show respect.
(2) **Ano kata** (not **hito*) **wa otaku no goshujin deshoo ka.**
    Might that person be your husband?

Do not use *hito* to refer to yourself. Example (3) is wrong.
(3) **Miura to iu hito desu.* (man introducing himself)
    lit., I'm a person called Miura.

In such a case, either use *mono,* the humble equivalent of *hito*, as in (4), or try a different construction, as in (5) or (6).
(4) **Miura to iu mono desu.**
    lit., I'm a person called Miura.
(5) **Miura desu.**
    I'm Miura.
(6) **Miura to iimasu** (or **mooshimasu**).
    My name is Miura. (lit., I'm called Miura.)

HONTOO NI 本当 really, truly

Hontoo ni (lit., "in truth") has three basic uses. First of all, it indicates that something actually happens.
(1) **Sonna koto ga hontoo ni aru daroo ka.**
    Do you think such a thing is actually possible?

Second, it is used as an intensifier indicating a high degree of some quality.
(2) **Yoshida-san wa hontoo ni shinsetsu da.**
    Mr. Yoshida is really kind.

In this sense, *hontoo ni* is similar in meaning to *totemo* "very" or *taihen* "very."

Third, it indicates the speaker's genuine sentiment.

(3) **Hontoo ni arigatoo gozaimashita.**

Thank you very much for what you did for me.

Although *jitsu ni* also means "in truth" or "really," it can be used only in the second sense above (Tokugawa and Miyajima, p. 364). In other words, although *jitsu ni* can replace *hontoo ni* in sentence (2), it cannot in sentence (1) or (3). *Hontoo ni* is also more conversational in tone than *jitsu ni,* which is mainly used in writing.

In informal speech, *hontoo ni* is very often shortened to *honto ni.*

HOSHII 欲しい **to want [something]**

Hoshii is an adjective used with nouns and the particle *ga.*

(1) **Okane ga hoshii.**

I want (*or* wish I had) money.

(2) **Atarashii kamera ga hoshii n desu ga, okane ga nakute kaemasen.**

I'd like a new camera, but I don't have enough money to buy one.

With *hoshii,* the subject is generally first person, as in (1) and (2) above. In questions, however, the subject is usually second person.

(3) **Kore hoshii?**

Do you want this?

With a third-person subject, *hoshigaru* "to want [something]" is used instead. *Hoshigaru* is a verb that takes the particle *o.*

(4) **Uchi no musuko wa atarashii sukii o hoshigatte-iru.**
Our son wants new skis.

Hoshigaru implies that the person who wants something expresses that desire verbally or otherwise.

Hoshii should not be used in polite requests. For example, if you happen to be visiting someone's house and would like to drink some water, don't say

(5) **Mizu ga hoshii n desu ga.**
I want some water.

Say one of the following:

(6) (a) **Omizu o itadaki-tai n desu ga.**
I'd like some water.

(b) **Omizu o itadakemasen ka.**
Could I (lit., Couldn't I) have some water?

(c) **Omizu o onegai-shimasu.**
May I have some water? (lit., I humbly request some water.)

Hoshii should not be used to ask someone of higher status whether he would like something. It is not a polite enough expression. If you want to ask someone higher in status than you whether he would like, for example, some coffee, you shouldn't say

(7) **Koohii ga hoshii desu ka.**

The following question would be much more polite.

(8) **Koohii de mo ikaga desu ka.**
Would you like some coffee? (lit., How about coffee or something?)

Unlike English "want," *hoshii* is not used with the dictionary form of a verb.

(9) **Kore o kau koto ga hoshii.*
I want to buy this.

With verbs, *-tai* is used instead of *hoshii*.

(10) **Kore ga kai-tai.**
     I want to buy this.

However, *hoshii* may be used with the *-te* form of a verb if the doer of the action expressed by the verb is not the speaker.

(11) **Kore o katte hoshii.**
     I want you to buy this.

When used this way, *hoshii* is synonymous with *morai-tai,* as in

(12) **Kore o katte-morai-tai.**
     I want you to buy this.

Neither (11) or (12), however, is a polite enough sentence if you are talking to someone higher in status than you. In that case, say *Kore o katte-itadaki-tai n desu ga* "I'd like you to buy this."

ICHIBAN 一番 the most

Ichiban, meaning "the most" or "the ——est," is accentless.

(1) **Ichiban ookii kuni wa Sobieto desu.**
     The largest country is the Soviet Union.

(2) **Watashi no uchi de wa otooto ga ichiban hayaku nemasu.**
     In my family, my younger brother goes to bed the earliest.

  This should be differentiated from ¯ı¯chi-ban, meaning "No. 1," which is accented.

(3) **Boku no kurasu de wa Ueda ga itsumo ichi-ban da.**
     In my class, Ueda is always the best student.

IE 家 house, home

Ie is very much like *uchi* "home, house" in meaning, but

there are some differences in usage. According to Matsuo et al. (p. 36), *ie* is more appropriate when one is discussing the home as an abstract concept or as the basic unit within the traditional family system. *Ie* is also preferred in legal references to a house as property.

According to Tokugawa and Miyajima (p. 35), there is a geographical difference between the words *ie* and *uchi*. Generally speaking, *uchi* is more common in the Kanto Region (where Tokyo is located) and the Chubu Region (where Nagoya is located); in the remaining regions, *ie* is the preferred form.

II いい **good**

Ii normally means "good, excellent," as in

(1) **Ano eiga wa ii desu nee.**
    That's a good movie, isn't it?

(2) **Mori-san wa ii hito da.**
    Miss Mori is a nice person.

What is confusing is that *ii* may sometimes mean "No, thank you" or "You don't have to," when used in the expression *Ii desu yo*. Suppose you ask someone *Shimashoo ka*, meaning "Shall I do it [for you]?" If he answers *Ii desu yo*, the sentence must mean "You don't have to" or "No, thank you." *Ii desu yo* in this sense is always pronounced with a falling intonation and is thereby distinguishable from *Ii desu yo* meaning "It's good, you know," which is usually pronounced with a rising intonation.

(3) A: **Ano eiga wa doo desu ka.**
       How is that movie?

    B: **Ii desu yo.** (rising)
       It's good.

┌ ┐
IIE いいえ **no**

Iie is most often used in response to a question to signal contradiction. In response to affirmative questions, therefore, *iie* corresponds to English "no," as in (1) below, but in response to negative questions it corresponds to "yes," as in example (2).

(1) A: **Wakarimasu ka.** (affirmative question)
    Do you understand?
    B: **Iie, wakarimasen.**
    No, I don't.

(2) A: **Wakarimasen ka** (negative question)
    Don't you understand?
    B: **Iie, wakarimasu.**
    Yes, I do. (lit., That's wrong. I understand.)

English speakers, if they equate *iie* with English "no," will have difficulty when *iie* corresponds to "yes." There are two possible solutions to this problem. First, stop equating *iie* with "no"; instead take *iie* to mean "That's wrong." Second (if the first method doesn't work), drop *iie* and just say the rest. For example, in the case of (2) above, *Wakarimasu* "I understand" alone would suffice as B's answer.

Iie is a formal word and is rarely used in informal speech (except sometimes by women). *Iya,* a less formal variant used by men, may occur in informal, as well as formal, speech. *Uun,* another variant, is very informal and occurs only between relatives or very close friends.

As shown in example (2) above, *iie* used as a response to a negative question usually corresponds to "yes." There are some cases, however, where *iie* used as a response to a negative question corresponds to English "no."

(3) A: **Genki-soo ni natta ja arimasen ka.**
    You're looking much better, aren't you!

B: **Iie, mada dame na n desu.**
   No, I'm not well yet.

The above question, though negative in form, is actually affirmative in spirit. What the question really means is "You're looking much better, and that's great!" Speaker B therefore says *iie* to show disagreement.

Iie may also be used as a response to a compliment, an apology, or an expression of appreciation.

(4) A: **Zuibun rippa na otaku desu nee.** (compliment)
       What a nice house you have!

   B: **Iie [, tonde mo arimasen].**
      lit., No, not at all.

(5) A: **Shitsurei-shimashita.** (apology)
       Sorry [for what I've done].

   B: **Iie.**
      Never mind.

(6) A: **Senjitsu wa doomo arigatoo gozaimashita.** (appreciation)

       Thank you for what you did for me the other day.

   B: **Iie [, doo itashimashite].**
      Not at all.

There are many situations where "no" might be used in English but *iie* cannot be in Japanese. The following are some of these cases.

1. *Iie* may not be used to signal prohibition. For example, if you notice that your little child is about to touch something dangerous, don't yell *Iie!* to stop him. Say *Dame!* "You mustn't!" instead.

2. At a meeting, if you want to express verbally your disagreement with a speech being made, don't yell out *Iie!* but say *Hantai!* "I disagree!" instead.

3. Don't use *Iie* to express surprise. In English, upon hearing bad or incredible news, you may react by saying

"No!" or "Oh, no!" In Japanese, say *Hontoo desu ka* "Is that true?" or, on more informal occasions, *E?* "What did you say?" If you discover something really alarming (for example, if you suddenly realize that your wallet is gone), don't use *Iie!* Say *Taihen da!* "Good heavens!" instead.

4. When playing tennis and your opponent's shot goes too long or too wide, don't say *Iie!* Say *Auto!* "Out!"

IKAGA DESU KA いかがですか How are you? How about such-and-such?

This is the Japanese question that comes closest to "How are you?" in meaning and is therefore used very often by Americans in Japan. But the fact is that Japanese speakers rarely use it in that sense. Although they ask this question when they visit a sick person or when they see someone who they know has been ill, they don't say it to someone they see all the time whom they assume to be well.

Ikaga desu ka, in fact, is probably used more often to mean "How about such-and-such?" For example, in situations where an American would say "Would you like some ice cream?" to a visitor, a Japanese would either ask *Aisu-kuriimu de mo ikaga desu ka* "How about ice cream or something?" or bring in some ice cream without asking any question at all. (See also OGENKI DESU KA.)

IKU 行く to go

Iku refers to movement away from where the speaker is at the moment of speech. If you are at home while talking

about attending school every day, you use *iku,* as in (1); if you are at school while talking about the same activity, you must use *kuru* instead, as in (2) below (see KURU).
(1) **Mainichi gakkoo e ikimasu.** (speaker not at school)
 I go to school every day.
(2) **Mainichi gakkoo e kimasu.** (speaker at school)
 I come to school every day.

The speaker's movement toward the addressee also requires *iku,* although in English the verb "come" would be used in that case.
(2) A: **Hayaku kite kudasai.**
 Please come right away.
 B: **Ima ikimasu** (not *kimasu) **yo.**
 I'm coming! (lit., I'm going!)

Like other verbs of motion, *iku* takes the particle *o* when the preceding noun indicates the place along which the motion takes place.
(3) **Kono michi o ikimashoo.**
 Let's take this road. (lit., Let's go along this road.)

IMA 今 now

The most common way of asking the time is
(1) **Ima nan-ji desu ka.**
 What time is it now?
Whereas, in English, "now" is usually left out, in Japanese, *ima* is more often used than not.

The prenoun use of "now" meaning "trendy" has lately been introduced into Japanese as *nau na,* and most recently *nau-i (!).*
(2) **nau na fasshon**
 the now fashion

The expression *nau na* seems to carry a new up-to-date quality that *ima* does not possess.

⌐IMOOTO⌐ 妹 younger sister

The use of *imooto* "younger sister" parallels that of *otooto* "younger brother" (see OTOOTO). In other words, what can be said about *otooto* on the male side can also be said about *imooto* on the female side. The female counterpart of *otooto-san* is, predictably, *imooto-san*.

IRASSHAI いらっしゃい Welcome [to our place]!

Irasshai (or its more formal version, *Irasshaimase*) is a greeting for welcoming a customer to one's establishment (e.g., a store, restaurant, inn, etc.) or for welcoming a guest to one's home. As you walk into a department store in Japan and reach the foot of the escalator on the main floor, you are destined to be greeted by the *esukareetaa-gaaru* (lit., "escalator girl") with a polite *Irasshaimase* and a bow.

IRU いる, 居る to be, to exist

Iru meaning "[someone] exists" takes an animate being (excluding plants) as its subject.
(1) **Tanaka-san ga asoko ni imasu.**
    Mr. Tanaka is over there.
(2) **Akai tori ga ano ki no eda ni iru.**
    There is a red bird on that branch.
  Iru contrasts with *aru* "[something] exists," in that the latter takes an inanimate subject (see ARU).

The only exception to the rule is when the subject is a vehicle (e.g., *kuruma* "car" and *takushii* "taxi") with a driver inside. *Iru* is used then instead of *aru*.

(3) **Asoko ni takushii ga iru kara, notte ikimashoo.**
There's a taxi over there. Let's catch it.

IRU いる, 要る **to need**

Iru meaning "to need" takes the particle *ga*.

(1) **Motto kami ga iru n desu ga.**
I need more paper. (In some contexts, "I'd like some more paper" might be a better translation.)

Iru, though similar in meaning to the English transitive verb "need," does not take *o*. The following sentence is therefore ungrammatical.

(2) **Motto kami o iru n desu ga.*
For some reason, *iru* is rarely used in the past tense.

(3) *?Okane ga ichiman-en irimashita.*
I needed 10,000 yen.

Most speakers would express this idea otherwise, as in the following:

(4) **Okane ga ichiman-en hitsuyoo deshita** (or **hitsuyoo ni narimashita**).
I needed 10,000 yen.

ISOGASHII 忙しい **busy**

As a rule, only persons, not things, can be *isogashii*.

(1) **Konogoro isogashikute komatte-iru.**
I'm so busy these days it's awful.

(2) **Sumisu-san wa mainichi isogashi-soo desu.**
Mr. Smith looks busy every day.

The following are therefore wrong.
(3) *Denwa ga isogashii desu.*
    The line is busy.
(4) *isogashii toori*
    a busy street
Instead of (3) and (4), one would have to use (5) and (6), respectively.
(5) **Ohanashi-chuu desu.**
    The line is busy. (lit., [My party] is talking.)
(6) **nigiyaka na toori**
    a busy (lit., lively) street

ISSHO 一緒 together

Issho, a noun, is most often used adverbially with a following *ni.*
(1) **Issho ni utaimashoo.**
    Let's sing together.

When the person together with whom someone does something is mentioned, the particle *to* is required, as in the following example:
(2) **Kyoo wa Suzuki-san to issho ni shokuji o shimashita.**
    Today I ate [together] with Mr. Suzuki.
Thus (3) and (4) have different meanings.
(3) **Minna issho ni utaimashita.**
    Everybody sang together.
(4) **Minna to issho ni utaimashita.**
    I sang [together] with everybody.

Since *issho* is a noun, if it is used adjectivally as a pre-noun modifier, *no* (not *na*) must be inserted.
(5) **Kobayashi-san to issho •ɔ hito wa dare deshoo.**
    I wonder who that person is who is with Miss Kobayashi.

‌ITADAKIMASU いただきます **I humbly accept**

Itadakimasu (lit., "I humbly accept") is a greeting regularly used at the beginning of a meal. It is an expression of gratitude for the food one is about to eat. To start a meal without this salutation is bad manners at home and unforgivable when visiting someone else's house.

Although at one's own home *Itadakimasu* is only used to start a meal, it may be used by a person visiting someone else's house to acknowledge some food or drink that does not necessarily constitute a meal. A polite visitor, for example, may say *Itadakimasu* just for a cup of tea.

Since *Itadakimasu* literally means "I humbly accept," it may also be used when accepting a present from a non–family member of higher status.

‌ITAI 痛い **painful**

Although *itai* is an adjective, it does not always correspond to English adjectives such as "painful" and "sore." Instead, it often corresponds to a verb (e.g., "[something] hurts") or a verb + noun (e.g., "have an ache").

(1) **Nodo ga itai.**
    I have a sore throat.
(2) **Sore wa itai.**
    That hurts.
(3) **Atama ga itai.**
    I have a headache.

   Itai is also used as an exclamation.

(4) **Itai!**
    Ouch!

   A variant of *itai* used only as an exclamation is *Aita!* "Ouch!"

‾| ITSU いつ When?

Ordinarily, to answer a question containing an interrogative word (e.g., *dare, doko, nani,* etc.), you have to listen for the particle that follows the interrogative so that you can use the same particle in the answer.

(1) A: **Dare** *ga* **kita n desu ka.**
       Who came?
    B: **Takagi-san** *ga* **kita n desu.**
       Mr. Takagi came.
(2) A: **Doko** *e* **iku n desu ka.**
       Where are you going?
    B: **Yuubinkyoku** *e* **iku n desu.**
       I'm going to the post office.
(3) A: **Nani** *o* **tabete-iru n desu ka.**
       What are you eating?
    B: **Hanbaagaa** *o* **tabete-iru n desu.**
       I'm eating a hamburger.

Itsu, on the other hand, often appears without a particle.

(4) **Itsu** (not **Itsu ni*) **kita n desu ka.**
     When did you come?

   In the answer to question (4), *ni* may or may not be used, depending on the preceding noun. Compare (5) and (6) below. Without *ni:*

(5) **Kinoo (Ototoi, Senshuu, Sengetsu,** etc.) **kita n desu.**
    I came yesterday (the day before yesterday, last week, last month, etc.).

With *ni:*

(6) **Ni-kagetsu-mae (Ni-gatsu, Too-ka,** etc.) **ni kita n desu.**
    I came two months ago (in February, on the 10th, etc.).

⌐ ‾| ITTE-IRASSHAI いっていらっしゃい Hurry home!

Itte-irasshai, which literally means "Please go and come

back," is a farewell most often used by someone seeing off a member of his own household. *Sayonara* "Good-by" should not be used in this case. The closest English equivalent would be *Hurry home!* but *Itte-irasshai* is used much more frequently; it is a well-established formula for everyday use.

Itte-irasshai may also be said to a person leaving his office or community on a trip. Don't use it unless you know the person is sooner or later returning to the same place.

In rapid, less careful speech, *Itte-irasshai* is regularly reduced to *Itte-rasshai*.

ITTE-MAIRIMASU 行ってまいります **I'm leaving**

Itte-mairimasu (lit., "I'm going and coming back") is an expression of leave-taking used by someone departing from his own home (or his office, town, country, etc.) on an errand or trip from which he expects to return sooner or later. *Sayonara* "Good-by" cannot be used in this case.

Whether *Itte-mairimasu* precedes or follows *Itte-irasshai* (see ITTE-IRASSHAI) is immaterial. It does not really matter whether the person leaving home speaks first and says *Itte-mairimasu* to someone staying at home, who then responds with *Itte-irasshai,* or the person staying at home speaks first and says *Itte-irasshai* to someone leaving, who then answers with *Itte-mairimasu.* Either way is acceptable.

A more informal version, *Itte-kimasu,* has lately become very widely used, especially among young people. It may not be too long before *Itte-mairimasu* becomes completely obsolete.

IYA いや **unpleasant, awful, detestable, nasty**

Iya means "unpleasant, awful," etc.

(1) **Konna tenki wa iya desu nee.**
This kind of weather is awful, isn't it!
Iya takes *na* before a noun.

(2) **Iya na hito desu nee.**
Isn't he a nasty man!
Iya is sometimes used to mean *kirai* "dislike."

(3) **Kimi wa anna nekutai ga suki ka mo shirenai keredo, boku wa iya (or kirai) da na.**
Maybe you like a necktie like that, but I don't like it.

Children and women might use *iya* by itself as an informal interjection to show annoyance when bothered by someone (a tickler, for instance).

(4) **Iya!**
Don't!

This *iya* must be clearly distinguished from the *iya* used by men as a variant (perhaps a slightly less polite variant) of *iie* "no." *Iya⌐* meaning "unpleasant" is accented on the second syllable, whereas ⌐*iya* meaning "no" is accented on the first.

(5) A: **Kyoo wa ame ga furu deshoo ka.**
Do you think it'll rain today?
    B: **I̅ya, furanai deshoo.**
No, I don't think it will.

-JI 時 o'clock

-*Ji* is attached to a numeral to indicate "o'clock," as in *ichi-ji* "1 o'clock" and *ni-ji* "2 o'clock." Whereas English "o'clock" is often left out (e.g., "It's two now"), -*ji* is never left out. The same is true of -*fun* "minute." In the following example, therefore, only (a) is correct for the meaning given.

(a) **Ima ichi-ji go-fun desu.**

(b) *Ima ichi-go desu.*
   It's 1:05 now.

JIBIKI 字引 dictionary

Jibiki used to be the only word meaning "dictionary" in spoken Japanese. *Jisho,* a more formal version, used to occur mainly in written Japanese. Nowadays, however, *jibiki* seems to be in the process of being replaced by *jisho* even in spoken Japanese. *Jiten,* an even more formal version, is mainly used to indicate a particular type of dictionary, as in (1), or as part of the title of a dictionary, as in (2).

(1) **wa–ei jiten, ei–wa jiten, gairaigo-jiten, akusento-jiten**
   a Japanese–English dictionary, English–Japanese dictionary, loanword dictionary, accent dictionary

(2) **Kenkyuusha Shin Wa–Ei Daijiten**
   Kenkyusha's New Japanese–English Dictionary

JIBUN 自分 self

Jibun is used only in reference to a human being or an animal.

(1) **Watashi wa jibun ga iya ni natta.**
   I've come to hate myself.

(2) **Jibun no koto wa jibun de shi-nasai.**
   Take care of your own (lit., self's) affairs yourself.

Unlike English "self," which can be attached to pronouns (e.g., "myself," "yourself," "himself"), *jibun* is never attached to "pronouns" such as *watakushi, anata,* and *kare.* One either uses *jibun* by itself, as in (1) and (2) above (which is usually the case in speech), or attaches the word *jishin* to a "pronoun" (e.g., *watakushi-jishin* "myself," *anata-*

jishin "yourself"). The use of *jishin,* however, occurs almost exclusively in writing.

Jibun de meaning "of one's own accord, for oneself, in person, by one's own ability" is not exactly the same as *hitori de* meaning "by oneself" (i.e., "unaccompanied"). Although, in some contexts, either *jibun de* or *hitori de* may be used, their meanings are slightly different, as in (3) and also (4).

(3) **Jibun de iki-nasai.**

Go yourself. (i.e., Don't ask anyone to go in your place.)

(4) **Hitori de iki-nasai.**

Go alone.

Sometimes, only one of them can be used. In (5), for example, only *hitori de* can be used.

(5) **Hitori de** (not *Jibun de) **sunde-imasu.**

I'm living alone.

JIKAN 時間 hour, time

Jikan, when attached to a numeral, means "hour[s]," as in *ichi-jikan* "one hour," *ni-jikan* "two hours," *san-jikan* "three hours," etc. In this case, *jikan* is accented on the first syllable, i.e., *-jíkan.*

When *jikan* is used without an attached numeral, it means "time."

(1) **Jikan ga amari arimasen.**

I don't have much time.

In this case, it is accentless.

According to Tokugawa and Miyajima (p. 238), *jikan* meaning "time" is different from its near synonym *toki* "time" in at least four senses. First, although both words may be used in the sense of "duration of time," *jikan* refers to a shorter length of time than *toki*. Compare the following sentences, both of which mean "time certainly passes by fast."

(2) **Jikan no tatsu no wa hayai mono da.**

(3) **Toki no tatsu no wa hayai mono da.**

In (2), a time span of just a certain number of hours within one day is the issue, whereas (3) is concerned with a much longer period of time, such as days, months, or years.

Second, *toki* may just refer to opportunities or occasions, but *jikan* never does. Compare the following:

(4) **Isogashikute ochitsuite shokuji o suru toki ga nai.**

I am so busy that on no occasion do I have a leisurely meal.

(5) **Isogashikute ochitsuite shokuji o suru jikan ga nai.**

I am so busy that I don't have time for a leisurely meal.

Third, a particular or definite point in time, as indicated by a clock, is *jikan* and not *toki*. In (6), therefore, *jikan* is correct, but *toki* is not.

(6) **Asa okita jikan** (not **toki*) **o kiroku-shinasai.**

Please record the time you get up in the morning.

Fourth, *toki* is regularly used to form clauses meaning "when such-and-such happens," but *jikan* is not. In the following example, therefore, only *toki* can be used.

(7) **Watashi ga soto e deta toki** (not **jikan*), **choodo takushii ga toori-kakatta.**

A taxi just happened to pass by when I went outside.

JIMUSHO 事務所 office

When American students of Japanese learn the word *jimusho,* they often start using it in Japanese whenever they would use "office" in English. For example, they might ask their teacher

(1) *Sensei no jimusho wa nan-gai desu ka.*

to convey the meaning "What floor is your office on?" A professor's office, however, is not *jimusho* but *kenkyuushitsu* (lit., "research room").

In fact, the use of *jimusho* is limited to a small number of occupations. Lawyers, accountants, and architects generally call their offices *jimusho,* but doctors do not. A student of Japanese should therefore check with a native speaker before using *jimusho* with reference to a specific type of office. (See also KAISHA.)

JOOBU 丈夫 healthy, robust, strong

Joobu may be used in reference to either persons (or animals) or limited kinds of objects. In reference to persons, it means "healthy, robust, strong."

(1) **Ano hito wa joobu de, metta ni byooki ni naranai.**

He is very healthy and rarely becomes ill.

Joobu cannot be used, however, to indicate good health over a very short period of time, e.g., one day, one week, or even one month. Just as it is wrong to say "*He is robust today" in English, we do not use *Kyoo wa joobu desu* in Japanese to mean "I am well today." In such situations, we use *genki* (see GENKI).

(2) **Kinoo wa byooki deshita ga, kyoo wa moo genki ni narimashita.**

I was ill yesterday, but I'm already fine today.

Joobu, in other words, is concerned with one's physical makeup rather than with one's temporary physical state.

When used in reference to objects, *joobu* may describe

only a limited number of things, including leather, fabrics, and products made of such materials.

(3) **joobu na kawa** (or **kutsu**)
strong leather (*or* shoes)
(4) **joobu na kiji** (or **fuku**)
strong fabric (*or* clothes)

KABURU かぶる **to put on, to wear**

Kaburu is limited in its use in that it is reserved for wearing things to cover the head.

(1) **booshi (beree, herumetto, etc.) o kaburu**
put on a hat (beret, helmet, etc.)

Occasionally, the item that covers the head may also cover the body.

(2) **Taroo wa futon o kabutte nete-iru.**
Taro is sleeping, pulling a blanket over the head.

KADO 角 **corner**

Corners such as street corners are *kado*.

(1) **Ano kado o magatte kudasai.**
Please turn at that corner.

In referring to boxes, bureaus, dressers, desks, and other angular things, Japanese makes a distinction between outside corners and inside corners. Outside corners are *kado,* but inside ones are called *sumi*. One therefore says:

(2) **Tsukue no kado ni atama o butsuketa.** (outside corner)
I hit my head against the corner of the desk.

(3) **Tsukue no sumi ni haizara o oita.** (inside corner)
I put the ashtray on the corner of the desk.

KĀERU 帰る **to return**

Kaeru means "to go (*or* come) back to the place where one belongs" (Mizutani and Mizutani, 1977, p. 38). Going back to one's house is one typical instance of such an action. To mean "to go home," the Japanese speaker therefore says *uchi e kaeru* (lit., "to return to one's home"), rather than *uchi e *iku* (lit., "to go home").

(1) **Koyama-san wa moo uchi e kaerimashita** (not **iki-mashita*)

Mr. Koyama has already gone home.

Although *kaeru* is often translated into English as "to return," it is different from "return" in that *kaeru* is a much more commonly used word than "return." While "return," at least intransitively, is not a conversational expression and is used mainly in written English, *kaeru* is a very common term in both speech and writing.

Since *kaeru* may mean either "to go back" or "to come back," the compound verbs *kaette-iku* "to go back" (lit., "to go returning") and *kaette-kuru* "to come back" (lit., "to come returning") are frequently used to specify the direction of motion.

(2) **Ueno-san wa go-ji-goro kaette-itta.**

Miss Ueno left [to go home] about 5 o'clock.

(3) **Musuko wa yuube zuibun osoku kaette-kita.**

My son came home very late last night.

(See also MODORU.)

KAIMONO 買い物 **shopping**

Although *kaimono* is usually equated with "shopping," these two are not the same. The difference becomes clear when one examines the dictionary definitions of these two terms. "Shopping" is defined as "the act of visiting shops and stores for purchasing or examining goods" whereas *kaimono* is defined as *mono o kau koto,* i.e., "the act of buying something." In other words, shopping does not necessarily end in a purchase, while *kaimono,* especially in *kaimono o suru,* involves a purchase. For example, sentence (1) below is correct, but (2) is not.

(1) I was out shopping all morning but came home without buying anything.

(2) **Gozen-chuu zutto kaimono o shita keredo, nani mo kawanai de uchi e kaetta.*
     lit., I did the shopping all morning, but came home without buying anything.

Sentence (2) would become correct only if one used *kaimono ni iku* "to go shopping" instead.

(3) **Gozen-chuu kaimono ni itta keredo, nani mo kawanai de uchi e kaetta.**
     I went shopping in the morning, but came home without buying anything.

KAISHA 会社 business company

Kaisha meaning "business company, firm" is used quite frequently in Japanese, in fact more frequently than its English counterparts. The reason is that it is often used in Japanese in situations where "office" or "work" would be used in English. In America, for example, a company employee who goes to work every day would not say "*I go to the company every day" but rather "I go to work (*or* the office) every day." In Japanese, however, *kaisha e iku* (lit., "to go to the company") is the most common expression to use in such a case. The Japanese equivalent of "He is at work (*or* the office)" is also *Ima kaisha desu* (lit., "I'm at the company") if the person in question works for a business company.

The Japanese word for "company employee" is *kaishain* (lit., "company member").

(1) **Ano hito wa kaishain desu.**

He is a company employee.

However, within or in reference to a specific company, its employees are called *shain* instead of *kaishain*. In (2) below, a company president is talking about an employee.

(2) **Ano shain wa nan to iu namae ka ne.**

What's the name of that [company] employee?

In other words, while *kaishain* represents an occupation and stands in contrast with other occupations such as *ginkooin* "bank employee" and *koomuin* "government employee, civil servant," *shain* indicates a position and stands in contrast with other positions such as *shachoo* "company president" and *kachoo* "section chief."

KAKARU かゝかゝる [it] takes, costs

Kakaru meaning "[it] takes, costs" is most typically used in reference to money or time. The preceding particle is *ga*.

(1) **Kono shigoto wa jikan ga kakaru.**

This job takes time.

(2) **Kodomo no kyooiku wa okane ga kakaru.**

Children's education costs money.

However, when lengths of time or amounts of money are the issue, *ga* must be dropped.

(3) **Kono hon o yomu no ni too-ka** (not *too-ka ga) **kakatta.**

It took me ten days to read this book.

(4) **Kuruma o naoshite-morau no ni dono-gurai** (not **dono-gurai ga*) **kakarimashita ka.**

How much did it cost to have the car repaired?

Actually, *too-ka kakatta* "it took ten days" in (3) is short for *jikan ga too-ka kakatta* "timewise it took ten days," and *dono-gurai kakarimashita ka* "how much did it cost?" in (4) is an abbreviation of *okane ga dono-gurai kakarimashita ka* "how much did it cost moneywise?" When *jikan* and *okane* are deleted, *ga* naturally goes with them—hence no *ga* in (3) or (4).

KAKU 書く **to write**

In English, "write [to someone]" is regularly used to mean "write [someone] a letter." In Japanese, on the other hand, the word *tegami* "letter" is usually included.

(1) **Kinoo Ueda-san ni tegami o kaita.**

Yesterday I wrote a letter to Mr. Ueda.

In Japanese, the act of writing something and that of drawing such things as a picture, a map, or a chart are considered alike. *Kaku* therefore means "to draw," too.

(2) **e (chizu, zu, etc.) o kaku**

to draw a picture (map, chart, etc.)

However, when *kaku* means "to draw," it is written in *hiragana* alone (i.e., かく); the *kanji* 書 is normally reserved for *kaku* meaning "to write" (i.e., 書く).

KAMAIMASEN KA 構いませんか **Do you mind?**

In English, to ask someone if you may do something, you say "Do you mind if I do such-and-such?" or "Would you mind if I did such-and-such?" In either case, the question is in the affirmative. The Japanese counterpart, however, is in the negative, i.e., *Kamaimasen ka,* which comes from *kamau* "to care, to mind."

(1) **Mado o akete mo kamaimasen** (not *kamaimasu) **ka.**
Do you mind (lit., Don't you mind) if I open the window?

The addressee then answers *Kamaimasen yo* "That's all right" or "I don't mind" if it is all right, and *Sumimasen ga akenai de kudasai* "I'm sorry, but please don't open it" or some such thing if it is not (but never *Kamaimasu).

Kamaimasen ka is another version of *Ii desu ka* (or, more formally, *Yoroshii desu ka*) "Would that be all right?" Sentence (1) above, therefore, can be restated as

(2) **Mado o akete mo ii** (or **yoroshii**) **desu ka.**
May I open the window? (lit., Will it be all right if I open the window?)

In this case, of course, the question is in the affirmative (although the meaning remains the same).

KAMINARI 雷 lightning, thunder

Although in English "lightning" and "thunder" are clearly distinguished, in Japanese both are often taken care of by one word, *kaminari*.

(1) **Tooku de kaminari ga pikapika yatte-iru.**
There are flashes of lightning in the distance.

(2) **Kyoo no kaminari wa zuibun yakamashii.**
The thunder is really loud today.

There are also, however, such words as *inabikari* and *inazuma,* both meaning "lightning." They can be used when the speaker wishes to refer to lightning specifically.

KANAI 家内 my wife

Kanai "wife" most typically refers to one's own wife. Though one could use *uchi no kanai* or *watashi no kanai* to mean "my wife," *uchi no* (or *watashi no*) is usually left out.

(1) **Kanai ga byooki na no de komatte-iru n desu.**

    I am being inconvenienced because my wife is sick.

    There are many other expressions that also mean "my wife," such as *nyooboo* and *waifu* (from English "wife"), both of which are informal, and *tsuma,* which is very formal and somewhat bookish (see TSUMA).

KANGAERU 考える to think, to consider

The semantic range of *kangaeru* and that of *omou* "to think" (see OMOU) overlap to a considerable degree, as in (1) through (3).

(1) **Shiyoo to kangaeta (or omotta) koto wa sugu shite-shimatta hoo ga ii.**

    It is better to do immediately what one thinks of doing.

(2) **Kimi wa sono koto o doo kangaeru (or omou)?**

    What do you think of that?

(3) **Watashi mo soo kangaeta (or omotta) n desu.**

    I thought so too.

    However, there are at least two differences between *kangaeru* and *omou.* First, *kangaeru* is more analytical. It is for this reason that forms of *kangaeru* must be used in (4) and (5) below.

(4) **Doo yattara ii ka kangaete-** (not **omotte-*) **kudasai.**

    Please think about how to do it.

(5) **Sono mondai wa muzukashikute zuibun kangaeta** (not **omotta*) **ga wakaranakatta.**

> The problem was so difficult I couldn't figure it out
> though I really thought hard.

Second, *kangaeru* does not need an object, whereas *omou*
does need one, whether explicit or implicit. In (6), therefore,
only *kangaeru* can be used.

(6) **Ningen wa kangaeru** (not *omou) **doobutsu da.**
Man is an animal that thinks.

KANOJO 彼女 she

Kanojo came into use during the Meiji era (1868–1912)
under the influence of Western languages and literature, as
the Japanese counterpart of "she," just as *kare* (see KARE)
was adopted as the "equivalent" of "he." The difference
between *kare* and *kanojo* is that while *kare* had existed in
classical Japanese with the meaning of "that person" or
"that thing," *kanojo* was a new coinage made up of *kano*
"that" and *jo* (another reading of the *kanji* for *onna*
"woman").

Kanojo was first used in written Japanese only, especially in Japanese translations of Western literary works.
Gradually it came to appear in original literary works as well.
Nowadays it is sometimes used in speech, too, although its
use is still quite limited. Sandness (pp. 85–86) points out
some interesting characteristics of *kanojo* as used in contemporary magazine articles: (a) a foreign woman is more
likely to be referred to as *kanojo* than is a Japanese woman;
(b) a woman is more likely to be called *kanojo* than is a man
to be called *kare;* (c) articles translated from Western
languages use *kanojo* more often than nontranslations; (d)
women who warrant deference, such as Queen Elizabeth and
Empress Nagako, are never referred to as *kanojo*.

The rule of thumb, in my opinion, is to avoid using *kanojo* in speech. When you do, never use it in reference to a person whose social status (on the Japanese scale, of course) is higher than yours.

KANSHIN 感心 admirable, praiseworthy

Kanshin, with the addition of *suru,* becomes the compound verb *kanshin-suru,* which is usually translated into English as "to admire," "to be deeply impressed by" and such. To be precise, however, *kanshin* and *kanshin-suru* tend not to be used in reference to persons higher in status than the speaker. Sentence (1) is therefore correct, but sentence (2) is not quite proper.

(1) **Ano ko no shuuji ga amari rippa na no ni wa kanshin-shimashita.**

I was deeply impressed by that child's superior calligraphy.

(2) *?Yoshida-sensei ga shuumatsu mo kenkyuushitsu de kenkyuu-shite-irassharu no ni wa kanshin-shimasu.*

I am deeply impressed by Professor Yoshida's studying in his office even on weekends.

This tendency is even clearer when *kanshin* is directed toward the addressee.

(3) Son: **Moo shukudai yatchatta yo.**

I've already done my homework.

Father: **Kanshin da nee!**

Good for you!

(4) Section chief: **Ano shigoto wa yuube tetsuya de yatte shimatta yo.**

I stayed up working all night last night and finished that job.

    Secretary: **Kanshin desu nee!*

In (3), the father's saying *kanshin* is correct because he is talking to his son, who is lower in status. In (4), however, *kanshin* is unacceptable because the secretary is talking to her superior. She should say

(5) **Taihen deshita nee!**

    That must have been very tiring!

KARADA 体 body

While the English speaker says "good (*or* bad) for the health," the Japanese speaker usually says *karada ni ii* (or *warui*), which literally means "good (*or* bad) for the body." *Kenkoo ni ii* (or *warui*), which literally means "good (*or* bad) for the health," may be used sometimes, but it is not as common an expression.

KARE 彼 he

Kare, which used to mean "that person" or "that thing" in classical Japanese, was adopted by writers during the early years of the Meiji era to represent the idea of English "he." First it was used only as a written form. Recently, however, some people have started using it in speech as well, as in

(1) **Kare wa kyoo byooki rashii.**

    He seems to be sick today.

    Kare in Japanese is far more restricted in use than "he" in English. There are at least two reasons for this. First of all, most sentences in Japanese have no explicit subject. Second, *kare* is used mainly by young people in informal speech. It is never used in speaking to a person of higher status in reference to another person of high status. A student talking to a teacher about another teacher, for example, should not use *kare;* he should either say *ano sensei* "that teacher" or name the teacher (e.g., *Yamashita-sensei*).

(2) Teacher: **Kimi no eigo no sensei wa dare.**

Who's your English teacher?

Student: **Yamashita-sensei desu. Ano sensei (or Yama-shita-sensei) no kurasu wa muzukashii desu.**

Mr. Yamashita. His (lit., that teacher's *or* Mr. Yamashita's) class is tough.

KARIRU 借りる **to borrow, to rent [from someone]**

Kariru often corresponds to English "borrow."

(1) **Saifu o wasureta kara, Ishii-san ni sen-en karita.**

Since I forgot my wallet, I borrowed 1,000 yen from Mr. Ishii.

Sometimes *kariru* corresponds to other English verbs.

(2) **Ano hito no karite-iru apaato wa zuibun ookii desu nee.**

Isn't the apartment he's renting huge!

(3) **Uchi no denwa ga koshoo da kara, tonari no denwa o karite denwa-gaisha ni kaketa.**

Since our phone was out of order, I used the neighbor's phone to call the phone company.

(4) **Toshokan ni hon o kari ni iku tokoro desu.**

I'm on my way to the library to take out a book.

Concerning example (2) above, English speakers should remember that *kariru* does not mean "to rent [*to* someone]." The word for this is *kasu* (see KASU). Example (3) demonstrates why Japanese speakers often make the error of saying in English "*May I borrow your telephone?"

Although *kariru* corresponds to a different English verb

in each of the four examples above, it maintains the same basic meaning: "to use something that belongs to someone else."

KASU 貸す to lend, to rent [to someone]

Kasu is the opposite of *kariru* (see KARIRU) and, as such, corresponds to various English verbs.

(1) **Terada-san ni gosen-en kashite ageta.**
   I lent Mr. Terada 5,000 yen.
(2) **Ooya wa kono uchi wa nijuu-man-en-ika de wa kasenai to itte-iru.**
   The landlord says he can't rent this house [to anyone] for less than 200,000 yen.
(3) **Chotto denwa o kashite kudasai.**
   Please let me use your phone.
(4) **Ano toshokan de wa firumu mo kasu soo desu.**
   I hear that library lets you take out films too.

Although *kasu* is represented by a different English verb in each sentence above, its basic meaning remains the same in all: "to let [someone] use [something]."

KAWA 川 river

"River" is defined as "a natural stream of water of fairly large size." *Kawa*, on the other hand, may refer to a stream of almost any size, wide or narrow. As Ogasawara (p. 129) points out, therefore, while "jump over a river" (instead of "stream") sounds strange in English, *kawa o tobikoeru* "to jump over a *kawa*" is perfectly acceptable in Japanese.

KAZOKU 家族 family

Kazoku means "family," as in

(1) **Nihon no kazoku wa chiisaku natte-kite-iru.**
    Japanese families have been getting smaller.
    Kazoku can also mean "family member."

(2) **Watashi ni wa kazoku ga go-nin aru.**
    I have five family members. (i.e., There are five in my
    family [excluding myself]).

Example (2) should be clearly distinguished from *Uchi wa go-nin kazoku desu* "Ours is a five-member family [including myself]." Example (2) also shows why some Japanese make the mistake of using "*I have five families" in English to mean "I have five family members."

KAZU 数 number

Kazu meaning "number" is used only when the amount is the issue.

(1) **Jidoosha no kazu ga hidoku fuete-kita.**
    The number of automobiles has increased tremendously.

Phone numbers and such serial numbers as license numbers are *bangoo,* not *kazu.*

(2) **Denwa-bangoo o oshiete kudasai.**
    Please give me your phone number.

To ask "what number," however, say *nan-ban,* not **nan-bangoo.*

(3) **Otaku no denwa-bangoo wa nan-ban desu ka.**
    What (lit., What number) is your phone number?

KEKKON-SURU 結婚する **to get married**

Students of Japanese whose native language is English often confuse *kekkon-suru* "to get married" and *kekkon-shite-iru* "to be in the state of having gotten married." The reason for this confusion is that, in English, "be married" not only means "be in the state of marriage" but is often used in the sense of "get married," as in "He was (*or* got) married yesterday." In Japanese, the distinction between *kekkon-suru* and *kekkon-shite-iru* is clearly observed.

(1) **Ano hito wa raigetsu kekkon-suru** (not *kekkon-shite-iru) **soo desu.**

   I hear he will be getting married next month.

(2) **Ano hito wa dokushin ja arimasen. Moo kekkon-shite-imasu** (not *kekkon-shimasu) **yo.**

   He isn't single. He's already married.

In English, one says "marry [someone]" or "be married [to someone]." In Japanese, on the other hand, *kekkon-suru* and *kekkon-shite-iru* take the particle *to*.

(3) **Sumisu-san wa Nihon-jin to** (not *o or *ni) **kekkon-shimashita** (or **kekkon-shite-imasu**).

   Mr. Smith married (*or* is married to) a Japanese.

KEKKOO DESU 結構です **That's fine**

Kekkoo desu is a politer and more humble variant of *Ii desu*. It is used, for example, as a response to a request.

(1) A: **Ashita ukagatte mo yoroshii deshoo ka.**

   May I visit you tomorrow?

   B: **Kekkoo desu yo.**

   By all means. (lit., That would be fine.)

Kekkoo desu usually occurs in affirmative statements. In (1), for example, if speaker B does not want speaker A to come tomorrow, he should not say *Kekkoo ja arimasen* (lit., "That wouldn't be good"), but something else, such as

(2) **Ashita wa chotto komarimasu ga.**

Tomorrow would be a bit inconvenient.

Kekkoo desu is also a polite way of declining a suggestion or an invitation.

(3) A: **Koohii de mo nomimashoo ka.**

Shall we have coffee or something?

B: **Kekkoo desu.**

No, thank you.

Although most Japanese would take *Kekkoo desu* in this case to mean "No, thank you," some might interpret it as "That would be fine." To avoid ambiguity, say *Iie, kekkoo desu* for "No, thank you," and *Kekkoo desu nee* for "That would be fine."

KESSHITE 決して by no means

Kesshite is used in a negative sentence to mean "by no means." Although it can occur by itself as a statement, it usually combines with a negative word to convey a strong negation. Using *kesshite* is like saying "I swear to you that such-and-such cannot happen."

(1) **Sonna koto wa kesshite arimasen.**

That is by no means possible.

(2) **Kare wa kesshite baka de wa nai.**

He is by no means stupid.

Equating *kesshite* with "never" is dangerous, for this equation can hold only as long as "never" is used in the sense of "absolutely not." *Kesshite* should not be equated with "never" meaning "at no time."

(3) **Sonna koto wa kesshite yurusenai.**

I shall never allow such a thing.

(4) **Hawaii de wa yuki ga furu koto ga nai**.

   It never snows in Hawaii.

In example (3), "never" corresponds to *kesshite* because "never" is used in the sense of "absolutely not." In (4), however, "never" means "at no time"; the corresponding Japanese version, therefore, does not use *kesshite*.

   Kesshite is mostly used in writing. In speech, it sounds formal; in informal conversation, use *zettai ni* "absolutely."

(5) **Sonna koto wa zettai ni nai yo.**

   That's absolutely impossible.

KIKU 聞く **to listen, to hear, to ask [a question]**

Kiku means "to listen, to hear," as in (1) and (2).

(1) **Maiasa rajio no nyuusu o kiku.**

   Every morning I listen to the news on the radio.

(2) **Tanabe-san ga byooki ni natta to kiite bikkuri-shita.**

   I was surprised to hear that Mr. Tanabe had gotten ill.

Note that while English "listen" is an intransitive verb and takes "to," as in "listen to the news," *kiku* is a transitive verb and takes *o;* e.g., *nyuusu (rajio, ongaku,* etc.) *o kiku* "listen to the news (the radio, music, etc.)." *Kiku* preceded by a sentence + *to,* as in (2), means "to hear."

   Kiku also means "to ask [a question]." The noun signifying the person to whom the question is directed is followed by the particle *ni*.

(3) **Sensei ni kikimashoo.**

   Let's ask the teacher [the question].

Sometimes *dare-dare* (i.e., "someone") *ni* (as in *sensei ni*) is followed by *nani-nani* (i.e., "something") *o*.

(4) **Junsa ni michi o kikimashita.**

   I asked a policeman the way [to a place].

When the word *shitsumon* "question" is used, *kiku* must be avoided. **Shitsumon o kiku* would be just as wrong in Japanese as "*inquire a question" would be in English. Use *shitsumon-suru* instead.

(5) **Sensei ni shitsumon-shimashoo** (not **shitsumon o kikimashoo*).

Let's ask the teacher some questions.

Kiku meaning "to ask" also occurs in the structure "question + *to kiku*."

(6) **Nan-ji desu ka to kikimashita.**

I asked what time it was.

KIMI 君 you

Kimi is more restricted in use than *anata,* which also means "you" (see ANATA). It is used only by men when talking either to a close friend or to someone of lower status (e.g., a teacher talking to a student). Although it is most often used in addressing males, females may sometimes be addressed as *kimi* (e.g., an executive talking to a female clerk, or a young man addressing his wife).

KIMONO 着物 kimono, clothing

Kimono has two meanings. First, in a narrow sense, it refers to kimono, i.e., traditional Japanese-style clothing. When it is used in this sense, as in (1) below, it is synonymous with *wafuku* "Japanese clothing," the only difference being that *kimono* is a more colloquial term than the latter.

(1) **Kyoo wa yoofuku o kinai de kimono o kiyoo.**

I think I'll wear a kimono today instead of Western clothing.

More broadly, however, *kimono* may refer to clothing in general.

(2) **Ofuro no ato de sugu kimono o kinai to kaze o hikimasu yo.**

If you don't put on your clothes right after a/the bath, you'll catch a cold.

My hunch is that this second use is on the decline, and that *kimono* in the sense of "clothing in general" is gradually being replaced by other words such as *fuku* "clothes." This is no doubt due to the fact that more and more Japanese wear Western clothes rather than kimono.

KINJO 近所 **neighborhood**

Kinjo means "neighborhood" in the sense of "vicinity."

(1) **Uchi no kinjo ni wa posuto ga nai.**

In my neighborhood there aren't any mailboxes.

Kinjo does not mean "neighborhood" in the sense of "locality." The use of *kinjo* in (2) is therefore wrong.

(2) **Koko wa modan na kinjo desu nee.*

This is a modern neighborhood, isn't it!

To convey the idea of the English sentence above, one would have to replace *kinjo* by another word, such as *juutakuchi* "residential district."

(3) **Koko wa modan na juutakuchi desu nee.**

This is a modern residential district, isn't it!

Although, in English, *in the neighborhood of* may mean "about," as in *The population of Tokyo is in the neighborhood of ten million, kinjo* is never used in that sense. Use *-gurai* (see GURAI) instead.

KIREI きれい **pretty, beautiful, clean**

Kirei has two basic meanings. First, it means "pretty, beautiful, lovely."

(1) **Kirei desu nee.**
Isn't she pretty!

(2) **Kirei na hana o arigatoo.**
Thanks for the beautiful flowers.
Second, *kirei* means "clean, neat."

(3) **Te o kirei ni arai-nasai.**
Wash your hands clean.

(4) **Motto kirei ni kaite kudasai.**
Please write more neatly.

It is extremely interesting that the ideas of cleanliness and beauty are expressed by one and the same word in Japanese. This is, however, not surprising when one thinks of the high regard Shintoists hold for cleanliness. (See also UTSUKUSHII.)

KIRU 着る **to put on, to wear**

Kiru means "to put on (*or* wear), on the body," usually by putting one's arms through sleeves (Soga, p. 281). The head and the limbs may be involved but the trunk must be the main portion to be covered. Nouns that may be used as the object of *kiru* are, for example, *kimono, yoofuku* "Western clothes," *wafuku* "Japanese clothes" (i.e., kimono), *uwagi* "jacket," *oobaa* "overcoat," *seetaa* "sweater," *shatsu* "undershirt," *waishatsu* "dress shirt," *reenkooto* "raincoat," *burausu* "blouse," *yukata* "informal summer kimono," *pajama,* "pajamas," and *sebiro* "men's suit."

(1) **Nihonjin wa konogoro taitei yoofuku o kite-iru.**
Nowadays the Japanese are wearing Western clothes most of the time.

(2) **Ono-san wa wafuku o kiru to suteki desu nee.**
Miss Ono looks terrific in a kimono, doesn't she!

Clothing and other wearable items not intended for the trunk of the body require other verbs, such as *haku, kaburu,* and *hameru,* depending on where and how they are put on. (See the entries for these verbs for more detail.)

As is the case with other verbs meaning "to put on," *kiru* refers to the act of putting on clothes, whereas the *te*-form + *iru* refers to the state of having put something on. Compare the following:

(3) **Soto wa samui kara, uchi o deru mae ni oobaa o kiru** (not **kite-iru*) **hoo ga ii.**
Since it's cold, you should put on your overcoat before you go out of the house.

(4) **Ano shiroi sebiro o kite-iru** (not **kiru*) **hito wa dare desu ka.**
Who's that man in a white suit?

KO 子 child

Ko, like *kodomo* (see KODOMO), means "child," but, unlike *kodomo,* it is rarely used without a modifier, especially in conversation. In sentences (1) and (2) below, for example, *kodomo* is correct but *ko* is not quite acceptable.

(1) **Kodomo** (not **Ko*) **wa kawaii.**
Children are cute.

(2) **Asoko ni kodomo** (not **ko*) **ga iru.**
There is a child over there.

When there is a modifier, however, *ko* is just as acceptable as *kodomo.*

(3) **ano (uchi no, ookii, genki na,** etc.) **ko** (or **kodomo**)
that (my, big, vigorous, etc.) child

KODOMO 子供 **child**

Kodomo is similar to English "child" in meaning in that it means both "child" as the antonym of "adult," as in (1), and "child" as the antonym of "parent," as in (2).
(1) **Nihon no kodomo wa konogoro ookiku natta.**
Japanese children have grown larger these days.
(2) **Watashi no ichiban ue no kodomo wa moo nijuu-go desu.**
My oldest child is already 25.
(See also KO.)

KOMARU 困る **to be at a loss**

Komaru may be translated as a great variety of English words, such as "be at a loss," "be troubled," "be distressed," "be embarrassed," "be in difficulty," to name a few. It basically refers to the unsure state of a person who has met a situation which he does not know how to handle.
(1) **Megane o nakushite komatte-iru n desu.**
I'm at a loss without my glasses. (lit., Having lost my glasses, I'm being inconvenienced.)
(2) **Ano hito wa konogoro kane ni komatte-iru rashii.**
It seems that he's hard up these days. (lit., It seems that he is in need of money these days.)
The informal past form *komatta* is often used adjectivally in prenoun position.
(3) **komatta mondai**
an embarrassing (*or* perplexing, deplorable, distressing) problem

Komatta in this case means that the problem is of such a nature that it troubles (embarrasses, distresses, etc.) the speaker or whoever is involved. Likewise, *komatta hito* most often means not "a person who became troubled" (although this is indeed possible), but "someone who troubles me" (Mizutani and Mizutani, 2, p. 73).

(4) **Uchi no shachoo mo komatta hito desu nee.**
   Doesn't our [company] president give us a big headache?

KOME 米 uncooked rice

Kome is what you buy at a rice shop, i.e., uncooked rice. Once it is cooked, it becomes *gohan* (see GOHAN) or *meshi* (see MESHI). In women's speech and men's polite speech, *kome* usually becomes *okome*.

KONDO NO 今度の next, this coming

"Next Sunday" meaning "this coming Sunday" is normally *kondo no nichi-yoobi,* rather than *tsugi no nichi-yoobi.*

(1) **Kondo no nichi-yoobi ni pikunikku ni ikimasu kara, issho ni irasshaimasen ka.**
   We are going on a picnic next (*or* this coming) Sunday. Would you like to join us?

   Tsugi no nichi-yoobi would mean "the following Sunday" or "a week from Sunday."

(2) **Kondo no nichi-yoobi wa tsugoo ga warui kara, tsugi no nichi-yoobi ni shimashoo ka.**
   Since next (*or* this coming) Sunday is inconvenient, shall we make it the following Sunday (*or* a week from Sunday)?

KONNICHI WA 今日は **Good day!**

Konnichi wa is usually equated with "Good afternoon!" but they are not identical. Although *Konnichi wa* is most often used in the afternoon, it is also used in the morning, and sometimes even in the evening.

Konnichi wa is not the same as "Hello!" either. Unlike "Hello!" *Konnichi wa* may not be said more than once to the same person on the same day. For example, if you have met someone in the morning and have exchanged *Ohayoo gozaimasu* with him, don't say *Konnichi wa* to him when you meet him again elsewhere in the afternoon of that same day. Just exchange a bow or say something like *Mata oai-shimashita ne* "Here we meet again."

Unlike *Ohayoo gozaimasu,* which can be said to anyone, *Konnichi wa* may be said only to outsiders, i.e., people who do not belong to one's own group (Mizutani and Mizutani, 1, p. 17). One does not therefore say *Konnichi wa* to a member of one's own household; nor is *Konnichi wa* normally exchanged between persons working in the same office.

Konnichi wa is a less formal greeting than *Ohayoo gozaimasu.* It is not proper, therefore, to use it to a person of higher status. On such occasions, use a substitute, such as talking about the weather (ibid.), e.g., *Oatsuu gozaimasu* "What a hot day!" (see OHAYOO GOZAIMASU).

In rapid, casual speech, *Konnichi wa* is often shortened to *Konchiwa.*

KONO-AIDA この間 **the other day, recently**

Kono-aida should not be confused with *konogoro* "these days" (see KONOGORO). In sentence (1), only *kono-aida* is correct, whereas in (2), only *konogoro* is correct.

(1) **Kono-aida** (not *_konogoro_) **Yoshida-san ni aimashita.**
I saw Mr. Yoshida the other day.

(2) **Konogoro** (not *_kono-aida_) **yoku Yoshida-san ni aimasu.**
I often see Mr. Yoshida these days.

Kono-aida and _senjitsu_ are more or less synonymous, but the latter is more formal. Some speakers of Japanese may also feel that _kono-aida_ can refer to a slightly more distant past than _senjitsu_. _Senjitsu_ can be anywhere between "two or three days ago" and "a week or two ago," whereas _kono-aida_ may range from "two or three days ago" to even "a month or two ago."

Kono-aida becomes _konaida_ in rapid familiar speech.

(3) **Ano eiga wa moo konaida michatta yo.**
I already saw that movie just the other day.

KONOGORO このごろ these days

Konogoro means "these days."

(1) **Yamashita-san wa konogoro futotte-kimashita ne.**
Mr. Yamashita has gotten a little heavier these days, hasn't he!

Konogoro (accentless) is different in meaning from _kono koro_ (accented on the next to last syllable) "about this time," which refers to a specific past time (see KORO).

(2) **Watakushi wa sen-kyuuhyaku-yonjuu-go-nen ni uma-remashita ga, chichi ga byooki ni natta no wa kono koro desu.** (example from Bunka-cho, p. 370)
I was born in 1945, and it was about this time that my father fell ill.

Strangely enough, we do not have such words as *_sonogoro_ or *_anogoro_, but only _sono koro_ and _ano koro_, both meaning "about that time" or "in those days." (For the semantic difference between _sono_ and _ano_, see ARE.)

KOOBA 工場 factory

Kooba is synonymous with *koojoo*. In fact, they are two different readings of the same characters. They are, however, not exactly interchangeable. *Kooba* sounds more informal than *koojoo*. In proper names referring to factories, *koojoo* is the norm. While *kooba* calls to mind a smaller, less than modern factory, *koojoo* conjures up the image of a larger, modern, well-equipped factory (Tokugawa and Miyajima, p. 159).

KOOEN 公園 park

In English, the word "park" brings to mind a spacious grassy area surrounded by trees. *Kooen* may refer to that kind of place, too, but it may also refer to a tiny public playground with swings and seesaws but without any greenery.

"Park" has a wider range of meaning than *kooen*. For example, whereas the former appears in such compounds as "ball park" and "amusement park," *kooen* cannot. "[Base] ball park" is *yakyuujoo* (lit., "baseball place"), and "amusement park" is *yuuenchi* (lit., "play-garden area").

KOOGI 講義 lecture

Academic lectures given as a course at a college or a university are *koogi*.

(1) **Mainichi Ogura-sensei no koogi ni dete-iru.**
    I attend Professor Ogura's lecture every day.

Public lectures on nonacademic topics are not *koogi* but *kooen*. *Kooen* can be on academic topics, but there are at least two differences between *koogi* and *kooen:* a *kooen* is (a) usually directed to a wider audience, and (b) generally a one-shot affair.

(2) **Kinoo wa kookaidoo de sekiyu-kiki ni tsuite yuumei na keizai-hyooronka no tokubetsu-kooen ga atta.**
Yesterday at the public hall there was a special lecture on the oil crisis by a well-known economic critic.

KOOHAI 後輩 one's junior

If a person enters, and graduates from, the same school or college that you do, but behind you in time, he is not a *tomodachi* "friend" (see TOMODACHI) to you no matter how close the relationship. He is your *koohai* (lit., "junior") instead, and you are his *senpai* (lit., "senior"). In Japanese society, which views human relationships in terms of higher and lower status, even one year's difference in time makes a crucial difference in terminology. Furthermore, a *koohai* must speak to a *senpai* more politely than vice versa (see SENPAI).

KOOKAI 後悔 regret

Kookai literally means "after regret," which explains why it can refer only to a sense of remorse, guilt, or self-reproach concerning a previous act.

(1) **Wakai koro sake o nomi-sugita koto o kookai-shite-imasu.**
I regret having drunk too much when I was younger.
Regret about something that has not taken place requires *zannen* rather than *kookai*. In example (2) below, therefore, only (b) is correct.

(2) **Byooki de ashita no pikunikku ni ikarenai**

(a) **koto o kookai-shite-imasu.*
(b) **no ga zannen desu.**

I regret not being able to go to tomorrow's picnic because of my illness.

One can feel a sense of *kookai* only about one's own acts and not about someone else's. In the latter case, *zannen* must be used. In example (3), therefore, only (b) is correct.

(3) **Musuko ga kootsuujiko o okoshita koto o**

(a) **kookai-shite-imasu.*
(b) **zannen ni omoimasu.**

I regret that my son caused a traffic accident.

If, however, the speaker feels directly responsible for his son's accident, *kookai* is the correct word.

(4) **Musuko ni kootsuujiko o okosasete-shimatte kookai-shite-imasu.**

I regret having caused my son's traffic accident.

Likewise, if "my son" is the person who feels guilty about his own deed, *kookai* is the word to be used.

(5) **Musuko wa kootsuujiko o okoshita koto o kookai-shite-imasu.**

My son regrets having caused a traffic accident.

Incidentally, note the use of *wa* in (5), as compared with *ga* in (3), and the difference in meaning between the two sentences. (See also ZANNEN.)

KORE これ this

Kore is used for referring to something near the speaker.

(1) **Kore wa kyoo no shinbun desu.** (speaker touching a newspaper)

This is today's paper.

In English, "this" is used in telephone conversations to

refer to oneself or to the person at the other end of the line.

(2) A: Who is this?

    B: This is John Doe.

In Japanese, on the other hand, *kore* cannot refer to the speaker or the hearer. (In polite telephone conversations, *kochira* "this side" is used to refer to the speaker, and *sochira* "that side" to the hearer.)

Kore, as a rule, cannot refer to a person directly. In English, one can introduce A to B by saying "This is Mr. A." In Japanese, however, **Kore wa A-san desu* would be inappropriate (unless the speaker is pointing to a picture of A). *Kore* should be replaced by *kochira.*

(3) **Kochira wa Suzuki-san desu.**

    This is Mr. Suzuki.

The only exception would be when you are introducing a member of your family (or someone of lower social status).

(4) **Kore wa uchi no musuko desu. Yoroshiku onegai-shimasu.**

    This is my son. I'd like you to meet him (lit., Please treat him favorably).

KORO こ ろ approximate time

Koro means "about the time when," and refers not to a specific point in time but rather to a less clearly defined length of time. Compare the following:

(1) **Haha ga byooki ni natta no wa watashi ga kekkon-shita koro datta.**

    It was about the time I got married that my mother became ill.

(2) **Haha ga byooki ni natta no wa watashi ga kekkon-shita toki datta.**

It was when I got married that my mother became ill. In (1), *koro* signals that "my mother" may have become ill either before or after the wedding, but in (2), because *toki* is used instead of *koro,* it is clear that she became ill immediately after the wedding.

When *koro* is used as a suffix to a noun that indicates a point in time, it usually becomes *-goro,* as in *san-ji-goro* "about 3 o'clock." (See also -GORO, KONOGORO, and TOKI.)

KOTAERU 答える **to answer**

Kotaeru has two basic meanings (although there are some other minor uses as well): to answer a question, as in (1), and to answer by saying *Hai!* when one's name is called, as in (2).

(1) **Shitsumon ni kotaete-kudasai.**
Please answer my questions.

(2) **Namae o yobarete "Hai!" to kotaeta.**
I answered, "Here!" when my name was called.

Answering a door, the telephone, or a letter cannot be *kotaeru.* In each of the following examples, (b) is correct, but (a) is not.

(3) **Dare ka ga nokku-shita no de, genkan ni**
| (a) **kotaeta.* |
| (b) **deta** (from *deru*). |

I answered the door because someone knocked.

(4) **Denwa ga natte-iru no ni dare mo**
| (a) **kotaenakatta.* |
| (b) **denakatta** (from *deru*). |

Although the telephone was ringing, nobody answered.

(5) **Tegami o moratte sugu** | (a) **kotaeta.* |
| (b) **henji o dashita.** |

I answered (lit., sent a reply) immediately after receiving the letter.

(See also HENJI.)

KOTO こと, 事 thing, matter, fact

Koto, like *mono,* is often translated into English as "thing." *Koto,* however, refers only to an intangible thing (i.e., an event, a fact, or an act) and thus contrasts with *mono,* which basically refers to a tangible thing.

(1) **Hen na koto ga atta.**

A strange thing (i.e., event *or* act) happened.

(2) **Hen na mono ga atta.**

There was a strange thing (i.e., object).

It is for the same reason that, in example (3), only *koto* is correct, while in (4), only *mono* can be used.

(3) **Omoshiroi koto** (not *mono) **o shitta.**

I learned something interesting (e.g., interesting news).

(4) **Depaato de takai mono** (not *koto) **o katta.**

I bought something expensive at the department store.

-KUN 君 (suffix attached to a name)

-Kun, like *-san,* is attached to someone's family, given, or full name. This suffix is mostly used by a male in speaking to or about another male, usually a friend or someone of lower status. A male college professor, for example, names a male student of his in this manner (e.g., Sakamoto-kun).

As a result of coeducation, however, female students have started using *-kun* in reference to male students, especially in informal conversations. This is but one of the many areas where the traditional male-female distinction is breaking down.

Unlike *-san*, *-kun* is normally not attached to occupation names (see -SAN).

KURU 来る **to come**

Kuru basically refers to movement toward the speaker.

(1) **Ashita mata kite-kudasai.**
    Please come [here] again tomorrow.

Unlike English "come," *kuru* cannot refer to the speaker's movement toward the addressee unless the speaker is with the addressee at the moment of speech, as in (2).

(2) **Ashita mata kimashoo ka.**
    Shall I come [here] again tomorrow?

If, for example, A is outside B's house and asks B to come out, B must respond by using the verb *iku* instead of *kuru*. He must call out (3b) instead of (3a) to indicate "I'm coming."

(3) (a) *Ima kimasu yo.*

    (b) **Ima ikimasu yo.**

Kuru, however, may refer to someone else's movement toward the addressee if the speaker identifies with the latter as in

(4) **Ueda-san ga otaku e kitara, yoroshiku itte-kudasai.**
    If Mr. Ueda comes to your house, please remember me to him.

If there is no such identification with the addressee, *iku* is used instead.

(5) **Ueda-san ga otaku e ittara, yoroshiku itte-kudasai.**
    If Mr. Ueda goes to your house, please remember me to him.

KUSA 草 grass, weed

"Grass" in English usually refers either to the kind of plant that is grown in a lawn or to the kinds of plants that are cut and dried as hay. The latter are *kusa* in Japanese, but the former is called either *shiba* or *shibakusa,* and never simply *kusa. Kusa* also refers to weeds, but when one wants to focus on the useless or troublesome aspect of weeds, *zassoo* is more appropriate. Study the following examples:

(1) **Kinoo wa ichi-nichi-juu niwa no kusa-tori o shimashita.**
   Yesterday I did the weeding in the yard all day long.
(2) **Kyoo wa shiba o karanakereba naranai n desu.**
   Today I must mow the grass (*or* lawn).
(3) **Kotoshi wa zassoo ga ookute komarimasu.**
   Weeds are rampant this year, much to my annoyance.

KUSURI 薬 medicine

In English, "medicine" most commonly refers to a medical substance taken orally. *Kusuri* has a much broader range of meaning. It refers not only to orally taken medicine but also to ointments, antiseptics, suppositories, eye drops, restoratives, and the like. Although *kusuri* most often refers to a substance that is good for the health, in a broader sense it may refer to any chemical. Even insecticides, for example, can be called *kusuri.* Kurokawa (p. 71) cites *gokiburi no kusuri* "roach killer" (lit., "roach medicine") as an example.

KUTSUSHITA 靴下 socks

Kutsushita in a broad sense refers to all kinds of socks. Some speakers, however, seem to differentiate between *kutsushita* and *sokkusu* (from English "socks"). Women's socks are often called *sokkusu* instead of *kutsushita,* while men's socks are generally *kutsushita.* Sports socks, either all white or white with colored stripes, are frequently called *sokkusu* whether they are worn by men or women.

KYAKU 客 visitor, guest, customer

Kyaku refers to a person who goes to someone else's place (e.g., house, store, office, hotel, theater) for a visit, for business, for shopping, etc. *Kyaku* is usually a written form; in conversation, especially in women's speech, the more polite *okyaku-san* is the norm.

(1) Housewife (to maid): **Okyaku-san ga kuru kara, kudamono de mo katte-kite-choodai.**
    Since I'm expecting a visitor, will you go out and buy some fruit?

At stores known for their elegance, the staff speaks even more politely by saying *okyaku-sama.* At such places, you may hear this over the PA system:

(2) **Okyaku-sama ni mooshi-agemasu.**
    Attention, please. (lit., I humbly announce to you customers.)

A passenger is also an *okyaku-san* from the standpoint of the person (or persons) providing the transportation. After all, a passenger is in a sense a visitor, too. A cab driver, for example, will often address a passenger in his taxi as *okyaku-san.* There is another word meaning "passenger," *jookyaku,* which is a written form. Sometimes *jookyaku no minasama* is used to address passengers on an airplane.

KYOO 今日 today

Kyoo means "today" in the sense of "this present day."
(1) **Kyoo wa ii otenki desu nee.**
   Isn't the weather beautiful today!

Although, in English, "this" is sometimes substituted for "today," as in "This is Sunday," in Japanese, *kore* (or *kono*) "this" does not replace *kyoo*. "This is Sunday" is therefore
(2) **Kyoo** (not **Kore*) **wa nichi-yoobi desu.**
Likewise, "this afternoon" is *kyoo no gogo,* not **kono gogo.*

Unlike "today," *kyoo* normally does not mean "this present time (*or* age)" although a more formal version, *konnichi,* often does express this meaning in written Japanese, as in *konnichi no Nihon* "today's Japan."

KYOODAI 兄弟 brother, sibling

Kyoodai has two meanings. In a narrow sense, it contrasts with *shimai* "sister," and refers to brothers only, as in *kyoodai-shimai* "brothers and sisters." This use, however, occurs exclusively in written Japanese. More commonly, *kyoodai* means "sibling," regardless of sex.
(1) **A to B wa kyoodai da.**
   A and B are siblings.
In (1), A and B might be both males, both females, or one male and one female.
(2) **Boku wa kyoodai ga san-nin aru.**
   I have three siblings.
In (2) also, the speaker might have any combination of brothers and sisters. The following example might be particularly puzzling to English speakers.
(3) **Boku no uchi wa san-nin-kyoodai da.**

The above literally means "My family is three siblings." What it actually means is, however, that the speaker is one of the three children in the family. In other words, he has two siblings, not three.

If one wishes to specify the sexes of one's *kyoodai,* the best thing is to say *otoko no kyoodai* (lit., "male siblings") for brothers and *onna no kyoodai* (lit., "female siblings") for sisters.

(4) **Boku wa otoko no kyoodai ga futari to onna no kyoodai ga san-nin aru.**

I have two brothers and three sisters.

There is one big difference between "sibling" and *kyoodai.* While "sibling" is not a colloquial expression, *kyoodai* is an everyday term used by anyone.

KYOOJU 教授 **professor**

Kyooju means "professor."

(1) **Ano hito wa Toodai no kyooju da soo da.**

I hear he is a Tokyo University professor.

Kyooju can also be used as a title (e.g., *Kimura-kyooju* "Professor Kimura"), but its use is different from the use of "professor" as a title in English. In English, someone called Professor Brown, for example, could be a full, associate, or assistant professor. In Japanese, on the other hand, to be called *Kimura-kyooju,* for example, the person has to be a full professor. If he is an assistant professor (the rank of associate professor does not exist in Japan), he is called *Kimura-jokyooju* (lit., "Assistant Professor Kimura") instead. This difference demonstrates how fussy the Japanese are about ranks and social standing.

The word *kyooju* sounds quite formal, and its use is usually restricted to written Japanese. In conversation, professors, like teachers, are all addressed or referred to as *sensei*.

(1) **Kyoo no Nomura-sensei no koogi wa omoshirokatta ne.**
Professor Nomura's lecture today was interesting, wasn't it!

-MA 間 (counter for rooms)

Rooms in houses are counted as follows: *hito-ma* "one room," *futa-ma* "two rooms," *mi-ma* "three rooms," *yo-ma* "four rooms," *itsu-ma* "five rooms," *mu-ma* "six rooms," *nana-ma* "seven rooms," and *iku-ma* "how many rooms." What is intriguing is the fact that -*ma* cannot be added to numbers over seven. This is probably due to the fact that Japanese houses rarely have more than seven rooms. For eight rooms or more, use *yattsu, kokonotsu, too, juuichi, juuni,* etc., without -*ma*.

Rooms in inns and hotels may be counted in the same manner as rooms in houses (i.e., by using -*ma*), but -*ma* is never used to count rooms in office or school buildings.

MAE 前 before, ago, front

Mae, when used as a time expression, means either "before," as in (1), or "ago," as in (2).

(1) **Ima shichi-ji go-fun mae desu.**
It's five minutes before 7 o'clock.

(2) **Go-nen mae ni kekkon-shimashita.**
I got married five years ago.
When used in reference to space, *mae* means "front."

(3) **Posuto no mae ni tatte-iru no wa dare desu ka.**

Who is that person standing in front of the mailbox?

Mae, however, may tolerate a greater space between the two objects involved than does "in front of." For example, it is perfectly all right to say in Japanese

(4) **Maru-biru wa Tookyoo eki no sugu mae ni aru.**

lit., The Marunouchi Building is right in front of Tokyo Station.

even though there is a large plaza between the building and the station. In English, however, one would more likely say

(5) The Marunouchi Building is right across from Tokyo Station.

MAJIME まじめ **serious**

Majime means "serious."

(1) **majime na kao**

a serious (*or* solemn) look

(2) **majime na gakusei**

a serious-minded student

Majime, however, is different from "serious" in that it cannot mean "important" or "giving cause for apprehension." One therefore cannot say

(3) **Infureeshon wa Amerika de ichiban majime na mondai desu.*

This sentence was written by a student of mine who was trying to convey the idea "Inflation is the most serious problem in America." He should of course have used *shinkoku* "grave" or *juuyoo* "important" as follows:

(4) **Infureeshon wa Amerika de ichiban shinkoku na** (or **juuyoo na**) **mondai desu.**

MESHI 飯 cooked rice, meal

Meshi, like *gohan*, has two meanings: "cooked rice" and "meal." The difference between *meshi* and *gohan* is purely stylistic, the former being used only by men in informal situations. According to Tokugawa and Miyajima (p. 387), the verb for "eat" would most likely be *taberu* for *gohan*, and *kuu* for *meshi*.

(1) **Gohan o tabemashita.**

   I ate some rice (*or* a meal).

(2) **Meshi o kutta.** (same meaning as above)

(See also GOHAN.)

MIDORI 緑 green

Green is normally *midori* although *ao* may be used in reference to certain items (see AOI). *Midori* seems to be gaining ground these days, so that the range of meaning of *ao* is becoming increasingly restricted to "blue." Youngsters in particular use *ao* less and less to mean "green," and say *midori* or even *guriin* (from English "green") instead. The latter is probably preferred in reference to Western-type things such as cars and Western clothing.

   In English, "green" often connotes envy, as the expression "green with envy" indicates. Japanese *midori* (or even *guriin*) has no such connotation.

MIJIKAI 短い short

Mijikai means "short," both temporally and spatially.

(1) **Fuyu wa hi ga mijikai.**

   Days are short in the winter.

(2) **Enpitsu ga mijikaku natta kara, atarashii no o kai-mashita.**

Since my pencil became short, I bought a new one.

Mijikai is different from "short," however, in that it cannot mean "short in height." To express the idea of "He is short," use (3a), not (3b).

(3) (a) **Ano hito wa se ga hikui.** (lit., His height is low.)

　　(b) **Ano hito wa mijikai.*

(See also HIKUI.)

MINA-SAN 皆さん everyone, all of you

Mina-san (lit., "everyone") is often used as the plural "you" and is more polite than *anata-tachi* "you (plural)."

(1) **Kondo mina-san o omaneki-shi-tai to omotte-iru n desu.**

I'd like to invite you folks one of these days.

(2) **Mina-san ogenki desu ka.**

Is everyone [at your house] well?

When you refer to your family, delete *-san* and use *mina.*

(3) **Okage-sama de mina genki desu.**

We are all well, thank you.

Mina can be replaced by *minna,* a more conversational variant. *Minna,* however, never takes *-san.* **Minna-san* is therefore a nonexistent word.

(4) **Mina-san** (not **Minna-san*) **ni yoroshiku.**

Please say hello to everyone [in your family].

MIRU 見る to see, to look, to watch

Miru is like "look" and "watch" in that it is intentional and not passive (Hattori, p. 198).

(1) **Kono hana o mite kudasai.**
Please look at these flowers.

(2) **Terebi o mite-imasu.**
I'm watching TV.

Miru is like "see" in that the object may or may not be stationary.

(3) **Kinoo wa Koorakuen e yakyuu o mi ni ikimashita.**
Yesterday I went to Korakuen Stadium to see some baseball.

(4) **Fuji-san o mita koto ga arimasu ka.**
Have you ever seen Mt. Fuji?

Unlike "see," however, *miru* cannot be used in the sense of "to meet and converse with." *Au* is the verb for that purpose (see AU). In (5), therefore, only (a) is correct.

(5) (a) **Ato de Sumisu-san ni au tsumori desu.**
(b) **Ato de Sumisu-san o miru tsumori desu.*
I plan to see Mr. Smith later.

Unlike "see," *miru* cannot mean "to visit and consult." Sentence (6) is therefore incorrect.

(6) **Isha o mimashita.*
I saw my doctor.

To indicate "visit the doctor for a consultation" in Japanese, you say *mite-morau* "to have the doctor look at [me]."

(7) **Isha ni mite-moraimashita.**
I saw my doctor. (lit., I had my doctor look at me.)

MISE 店 store

Mise has a broader range of meaning than English "store." *Mise* can refer not only to stores but also to such places as restaurants, teahouses, coffee shops, and even gas stations.

(1) A: **Kono kissaten wa konde-imasu nee.**
This coffee shop is crowded, isn't it!

B: **Soo desu nee. Motto suite-iru mise o sagashimashoo.**
   It is, isn't it! Let's look for a less crowded one.

(2) A: **Ano resutoran wa tsubureta soo desu yo.**
   That restaurant has gone bankrupt, I hear.

B: **Soo desu ka. Sekkaku ii mise datta no ni nee.**
   Has it? Too bad; it was such a nice place.

MIZU 水 [cold] water

Mizu is different from "water" in that it does not refer to hot water. In Japanese, hot water is referred to by an entirely different word, *yu,* or more commonly, *oyu* (see OYU). Example (1) below is therefore correct, but sentence (2) is incorrect.

(1) **Nodo ga kawaita kara, mizu o nonda.**
   I drank some [cold] water because I was thirsty.

(2) **atsui mizu*
   lit., hot water

To refer to really cold water, one may say

(3) **tsumetai mizu**
   very cold water

which is not redundant.

Drinking water may be referred to not only as *mizu* but also, when served very cold, as *ohiya* or *aisu-wootaa* (from English "ice water"). (This last variant, however, is used only at Western-style restaurants and coffee shops.) Non-drinking cold water can be called only *mizu.*

MODORU 戻る to return, to go back, to come back, to turn back

Modoru is often synonymous with *kaeru* (see KAERU).

(1) **Roku-ji-goro modorimasu.**

He'll be back about six.

In sentence (1), *modorimasu* may be replaced by *kaeri-masu*. There are, however, at least three important differences between *modoru* and *kaeru*. First, *modoru* is sometimes used as an antonym of *susumu* "to go forward," but *kaeru* is not used in this way.

(2) **Michi ga konde-ite saki e susumenai kara, ushiro e modorimashoo** (not **kaerimashoo*).

Since the street is so crowded, we can't go forward; let's go back.

Second, sometimes *kaeru* focuses on "leaving" rather than "getting back," while *modoru* focuses on "getting back." For example, if you call Mr. Watanabe's office and are told *Moo kaerimashita,* it simply means "He has already left here to go home."

Third, *kaeru* implies "going back to where one belongs (e.g., one's country or home)," whereas *modoru* implies "going back to and arriving where one was before" (Shibata et al., pp. 142–43). In example (3), therefore, only *modoru* would be correct.

(3) **koosaten ni modoru** (not **kaeru*)

to return to the intersection

In this case, *kaeru* is wrong because an intersection is not where a pedestrian (*or* a driver) belongs.

MOSHIMOSHI もしもし **Hello**

Moshimoshi is the Japanese equivalent of "Hello" used at the beginning of a telephone conversation. In Japanese, however, as Jorden (1, p. 194) explains, "it is the person who places the call who says *Moshimoshi* first; he speaks when he hears a click at the other end of the line."

(1) **Moshimoshi, kochira wa Suzuki desu ga, Takahashi-san wa irasshaimasu ka.**

Hello, this is Suzuki. Is Mr. Takahashi there, please?

Moshimoshi may also be used to attract a stranger's attention. For example, if you see a stranger drop something, you call out *Moshimoshi!* to catch his attention. However, if used at a restaurant or a store to get service, it will probably sound too formal. In that case, say *Onegai-shimasu* or *Chotto!* instead (see CHOTTO and ONEGAI-SHIMASU).

NADO など **and so on, and the like**

Nado is often the equivalent of "and so on."

(1) **Watashi wa ringo, orenji, momo nado ga suki desu.**

I like apples, oranges, peaches, and so on.

Nado may be used in conjunction with *ya,* which is inserted between the items cited.

(2) **Watashi wa ringo ya, orenji ya, momo nado ga suki desu.**

In (1) and (2), *nado* may be replaced by *nanka* (which also means "and so on"), as in (3) and (4), the only difference being that *nanka* makes the sentences more conversational.

(3) **Watashi wa ringo, orenji, momo nanka ga suki desu.**

(4) **Watashi wa ringo ya, orenji ya, momo nanka ga suki desu.**

Actually, since *ya* by itself implies "and things like that," neither *nado* nor *nanka* is really necessary in this case.

(5) **Watashi wa ringo ya, orenji ya, momo ga suki desu.**

Another use of *nado* (and *nanka*) is to provide an illustration to substantiate what precedes.

(6) **Konogoro wa nan de mo takaku natta. Gasorin nado (or nanka) toku ni takai.**

These days everything has gotten expensive. Gasoline, for example, is particularly expensive.

(7) **Kyoo wa isogashikute tegami nado** (or **nanka**) **kaku hima wa nai.**

I'm so busy today I have no time to write things like letters.

It is of course possible to be more direct and specific by using *o* instead of *nado.*

(8) **Kyoo wa isogashikute tegami o kaku hima wa nai.**

I'm so busy today I have no time to write letters.

In Japanese, however, one often prefers to be less direct and specific. Although (8) is of course correct, many speakers would prefer to use *nado* (or *nanka*) instead of *o,* as in (7) above. There are many other expressions in Japanese that help make statements less direct and less specific, such as *mo, -tari, bakari,* and *hodo* (Kunihiro, p. 37), and these are the words that lend Japanese its particular flavor.

NAKUNARU 亡くなる **to pass way**

Shinu is the most direct way of saying "to die," as in *Shinu no wa iya da* "I don't want to die." However, just as English speakers often say "pass away," avoiding the word "die," Japanese speakers frequently use *nakunaru* (lit., "to disappear") as a euphemism for *shinu. Nakunaru* is usually used in reference to people outside the speaker's family, but it may be used in reference to one's own relatives, too.

(1) **Tamura-san no otoo-san ga nakunatta to kiite odoroita.**

I was surprised to hear Mr. Tamura's father is dead.

(2) **Chichi ga nakunatte sugu sooshiki ga atta.**

Immediately after my father died, there was a funeral.

However, *nakunaru* is never used in reference to oneself. Use *shinu* in that case.

(3) **Watashi ga shindara** (not **nakunattara*) **kodomo-tachi wa doo suru daroo.**

What would happen to my children if I died?

The honorific form of *nakunaru* is *onakunari ni naru,* a term which should never be used in reference to one's own family.

(4) **Kono tabi wa otooto-san ga onakunari ni natta soo de** . . .
I'm sorry to hear that your younger brother has passed away. (lit., This time I hear that your younger brother has passed away . . .)

NAOSU 直す **to correct, to repair, to cure**

Naosu basically means "to make [something] right" and is used to mean "to repair, to correct, to cure."

(1) **terebi (tokei, kuruma,** etc.**) o naosu**
to repair a TV (watch, car, etc.)

(2) **machigai (sakubun, bun,** etc.**) o naosu**
to correct errors (compositions, sentences, etc.)

(3) **byooki (byoonin, kaze,** etc.**) o naosu**
to cure an illness (sick person, cold, etc.)

Thus, *naosu* has a much wider range of usage than either *shuuri-suru* or *shuuzen-suru,* both of which can only mean "to repair." *Shuuri-suru* or *shuuzen-suru* can therefore replace *naosu* in (1) above, but not in (2) or (3). *Shuuri-suru* and *shuuzen-suru* are synonymous and can be used more or less interchangeably. Tokugawa and Miyajima (p. 194) suggest, however, that *shuuzen-suru* might sound a little more dated than *shuuri-suru.*

NARAU 習う **to study, to take lessons**

Although *narau* is often equated with "learn" by American students of Japanese, it is more like "study" in the sense that it does not imply mastery as does "learn." (1) and (2) below are therefore correct, but (3) is not.

(1) **Uchi no musume wa ima piano o naratte-imasu.**
My daughter is taking piano lessons.

(2) **Eigo wa roku-nen mo gakkoo de naraimashita ga, joozu ni narimasen deshita.**
I studied English for six years in school but I never became good at it.

(3) *Aoki-san wa san-nen Amerika ni ita aida ni eigo o hitori de ni naraimashita.*
Mr. Aoki learned English without effort during his three-year stay in America.

To make (3) correct, *naraimashita* must be replaced by *oboemashita* "learned" (see OBOERU).

(4) **Aoki-san wa san-nen Amerika ni ita aida ni eigo o hitori de ni oboemashita.**

A student of mine once wrote sentence (5) below, with the intended meaning "It goes without saying that Japanese too can learn English."

(5) *Nihonjin de mo eigo ga naraeru koto wa iu made mo nai.*

Of course, he should have used *oboerareru* "can learn" instead of *naraeru* "can take lessons."

Narau and *benkyoo-suru* are often interchangeable, as below.

(6) **Daigaku de Nihongo o naratte-imasu** (or **benkyoo-shite-imasu**).
I am studying Japanese in college.

There are, however, at least three differences between the two verbs. First of all, *narau* implies the presence of a teacher while *benkyoosuru* does not.

(7) **Nihongo o naratte-imasu.**
(8) **Nihongo o benkyoo-shite-imasu.**

Although both (7) and (8) mean "I am studying Japanese," the speaker in (7) is presumably taking a course somewhere or taking lessons from a tutor, while the speaker in (8) might be just trying to teach himself.

Second, *narau* has to have an object while *benkyoo-suru* does not. Sentence (9) is therefore incorrect unless preceded by a sentence which specifies the object of studying, while sentence (10) is correct by itself.

(9) **Nishio-san wa naratte-imasu.*
    Mr. Nishio is studying [what?].

(10) **Nishio-san wa benkyoo-shite-imasu.**
    Mr. Nishio is studying.

Third, *narau* may be used for academic subjects as well as nonacademic skills, while *benkyoo-suru* is normally reserved for academic subjects only. When *benkyoo-suru* is used for nonacademic skills, it connotes a very serious endeavor. In (11), for example, one would most normally use *narau*. If, however, *benkyoo-suru* were used, it would connote that the speaker was taking lessons from a master carpenter perhaps with a view to making an occupation of carpentry. If carpentry is meant to be a hobby, the use of *benkyoo-suru* would indicate a very serious hobby. *Narau* has no such connotation.

(11) **Daiku-shigoto o naratte-imasu.**
    I am taking lessons in carpentry.

NARUHODO なるほど **I see**

Naruhodo means "I see" in the sense of "I see what you say is right." It is most often used as a response to an explanation given by someone. The implication is "Why didn't I think of it?"

(1) A: **Kono mado ga akanai n desu ga.**
    I can't seem to open this window.
   B: **Koo sureba ii n desu yo.**
    This is all you have to do.
   A: **Aa, naruhodo.**
    Oh, I see.

NERU 寝る **to go to bed, to sleep, to fall asleep, to lie down**

Neru has three meanings: "to go to bed," as in example (1) below; "to sleep, to fall asleep," as in (2); and "to lie down," as in (3).

(1) **Maiban juuichi-ji-goro nemasu.**
    I go to bed about 11 o'clock every night.
(2) **Maiban hachi-jikan nereba juubun deshoo.**
    If you sleep eight hours a night, it should be enough.
(3) **Nenagara hon o yomu to me ni yoku arimasen yo.**
    If you read lying down, it's not good for your eyes.

For each of these meanings, there is a synonym for *neru*: *toko ni hairu* "to get into one's bed," *nemuru* "to sleep, to fall asleep," and *yoko ni naru* "to lie down." But *neru* has a much wider range of meaning than any of these.

NIHONJIN 日本人 **a Japanese**

In English, "Japanese" means both "a Japanese" and "the Japanese language." *Nihonjin,* on the other hand, only means "a Japanese." (*Nihongo* is of course the word for "the Japanese language.") In fact, *Nihonjin* has a very narrow meaning, i.e., "a Japanese national." A Japanese–American, therefore, is not a *Nihonjin*. Japanese who have emigrated to other countries and have acquired citizenship in those countries—as well as their offspring, such as *nisei* and *sansei*—are referred to as *Nikkeijin* "person[s] of Japanese origin."

When *Nihonjin* is written in *kanji* (i.e., 日本人), the last character is the one for *hito* (人). Since *hito* is not an honorific expression, *Nihonjin* is not either. Upon meeting a Japanese-looking stranger, therefore, it is not courteous to use *Nihonjin desu ka* to mean "Are you a Japanese?" It is better to ask *Nihon no kata desu ka*, using *kata,* the honorific counterpart of *hito.*

NIKU 肉 flesh, meat

In English, "meat" and "flesh" are two different words, but in Japanese, *niku* takes care of both meanings.

(1) **Ano hito wa hone bakari de, niku ga nai.**
He is all bones and no flesh.

(2) **Konogoro no kodomo wa sakana yori niku no hoo ga suki desu.**
Kids these days prefer meat to fish.

NOMU 飲む to drink

Although *nomu* is often equated with "drink," it actually means "to take something orally without chewing" (Suzuki, p. 19). It is therefore used in reference to not only drinks but also orally taken medicine, and cigarette smoke. It may correspond to other English verbs besides "drink," depending on the object.

(1) **biiru o nomu**
to drink beer

(2) **kusuri o nomu**
    to take medicine
(3) **tabako o nomu**
    to smoke [a cigarette]
(4) **tsuba o nomu**
    to swallow saliva

NOROI のろい slow

Unlike *osoi* (see OSOI), which means both "late" and "slow," *noroi* can only mean "slow." When *osoi* is used in the sense of "slow," however, there is still a difference in connotation between the two words.

(1) **Ano hito wa aruku no ga** | (a) **osoi.** |
                                    | (b) **noroi.** |

He walks slowly.

Sentence (1a) is just an objective statement whereas (1b) implies that the speaker disapproves of that person's slowness (Tokugawa and Miyajima, p. 72).

NORU 乗る to get on, to get into [a vehicle]

While, in English, prepositions following "get" vary, depending on the means of transportation (e.g., "get on the bus," "get into a cab"), in Japanese, the particle used with *noru* is always *ni,* no matter what type of vehicle is in question.

(1) (a) **kuruma** (or **takushii**) **ni noru**
        to get into a car (*or* taxi)
    (b) **basu** (or **densha**) **ni noru**
        to get on a bus (*or* train)

Noru usually refers to the act of getting on or into a vehicle.

(2) **Kisha ga demasu kara, hayaku notte-kudasai.**
The train is leaving; please get on board immediately.

To refer to the act of traveling by some means of transportation, say *notte iku.* The particle used is still the same, that is, *ni.*

(3) **Mainichi kaisha made basu ni notte ikimasu.**
Every day I take the bus to the office.

If, however, *notte* is deleted from sentence (3), the particle has to be changed to *de.*

(4) **Mainichi kaisha made basu de ikimasu.**
Every day I go to the office by bus.

NUGU 脱ぐ **to take off [clothing]**

Whereas the act of putting on clothing requires various verbs such as *kiru, kaburu,* and *haku,* depending on what one puts on, the act of taking off clothing is often taken care of by one verb, *nugu.*

(1) (a) **uwagi o kiru**
to put on a jacket
   (b) **uwagi o nugu**
to take off a jacket
(2) (a) **booshi o kaburu**
to put on a hat
   (b) **booshi o nugu**
to take off a hat
(3) (a) **kutsu o haku**
to put on shoes
   (b) **kutsu o nugu**
to take off shoes

Other verbs meaning "to put on [clothing]" however, do not match up with *nugu,* but with *toru* or *hazusu* instead.

(4) (a) **nekutai o shimeru (or suru)**
    to put on a tie
   (b) **nekutai o toru**
    to take off a tie
(5) (a) **tokei o hameru (or suru)**
    to put on a [wrist] watch
   (b) **tokei o toru (or hazusu)**
    to take off a [wrist] watch
(6) (a) **megane o kakeru**
    to put on glasses
   (b) **megane o toru (or hazusu)**
    to take off glasses

NURUI ぬるい lukewarm

Nurui is as a rule used with reference to liquids to mean "not hot enough." That is why (1b) is wrong.

(1) (a) **nurui koohii (ocha, ofuro,** etc.)
    lukewarm coffee (tea, bath, etc.)
   (b) **nurui gohan (supagettii, piza,* etc.)
    ? lukewarm rice (spaghetti, pizza, etc.)

Sometimes, *nurui* means "not cold enough" in reference to liquids.

(2) **nurui biiru**
   lukewarm beer

When used figuratively, "lukewarm" means "half-hearted," as in "a lukewarm handshake." On the other hand, *nurui,* when used figuratively, does not mean "half-hearted," but "not strict enough."

(3) **Sonna nurui yarikata wa dame da.**

Such a measure is not strict enough and is therefore no good.

This figurative use of *nurui,* however, is probably not as common as *tenurui,* which also means "not strict enough."

⌐OBOERU⌐ 覚える **to commit something to memory, to learn**

Oboeru means "to commit something to memory," and therefore "to learn."

(1) **Hayaku Nihongo o oboe-tai desu.**
I'd like to learn Japanese as soon as possible.

(2) **Mainichi kanji o gojuu mo oboeru no wa muri deshoo.**
It might be too difficult to learn 50 Chinese characters a day.

To express the idea of "retaining something that has been committed to memory," one has to say *oboete-iru* rather than *oboeru.* American students of Japanese often make the error of identifying *oboeru* with "remember" and make sentences such as (3), but (3) is a misrepresentation of (4), and cannot mean "I don't remember his name."

(3) **Ano hito no namae wa oboemasen.*

(4) **Ano hito no namae wa oboete-imasen.**
I don't remember his name.

Sentence (3) can be correct only in the sense of "I won't (i.e., I refuse to) commit his name to memory."

Oboeru cannot mean "to bring back from memory," either. For that one needs *omoidasu* (see OMOIDASU).

ODAIJI NI お大事に **Please take care [of yourself]**

Odaiji ni is an expression of sympathy directed to someone who is ill or whose family member is ill. Although its literal meaning is "Take care of yourself," it is uttered in the same spirit as the English expression "I hope you (he, she, etc.) will get well soon."

(1) A: **Konogoro koshi ga itakute komatte-iru n desu.**

I've been bothered by a lower-back pain lately.

B: **Ikemasen nee. Odaiji ni.**

I'm sorry to hear that. Please take care of yourself.

In English, "Take care" is sometimes used as a farewell meaning "Good-by." *Odaiji ni,* on the other hand, is not used as a farewell unless the speaker knows that either the addressee or a member of the latter's family is ill.

OFURO おふろ bath

Ofuro, which is more often used than the plain form *furo,* means "bath" or "bathtub." "Take a bath" is *ofuro ni hairu* or *ofuro o abiru.* Sometimes *oyu* meaning "hot water" (see OYU) is used instead of *ofuro,* as in *oyu ni hairu.* "Get out of the bath" is either *ofuro o* (or *kara*) *deru,* or *ofuro kara agaru.* The reason *agaru* (lit., "to go up") is used is that, in Japan, after a bath one steps up from the bathroom to the anteroom where one's clothing was removed and left before the bath.

Ofuro does not refer to a room with a bathtub. Such a room is *ofuroba* (lit., "bath place") or, if it is a Western-style bathroom with a Western-style bathtub, *basuruumu* (from English "bathroom").

In English, "bathroom" serves as a euphemism for "toilet" and is used even when there is no bathtub in the room (e.g., "May I use your bathroom?"). *Ofuro,* on the other hand, can never be used to mean "toilet." For that purpose, say *otearai* or *toire* (from English "toilet").

(1) **Chotto oterai** (or **toire**) **o haishaku-sasete-kudasai.**
Please let me use your bathroom.

OGENKI DESU KA お元気ですか **Are you well? How are you?**

Although *Ogenki desu ka* "Are you well?" is sometimes taught in Japanese language textbooks for English speakers as the "equivalent" of "How are you?", the frequency of its usage is far below that of "How are you?" One does not indiscriminately direct the question *Ogenki desu ka* to everyone one encounters. In English, "How are you?" has almost been reduced to the status of a greeting, and it often serves merely as another way of saying "Hi!" *Ogenki desu ka,* on the other hand, has remained a genuine question and is reserved for someone one has not seen for a long time.

OHAYOO GOZAIMASU お早ようございます **Good morning!**

Ohayoo gozaimasu is a greeting exchanged between persons (whether or not they are members of the same family) when they meet in the morning. It may be shortened to *Ohayoo* in addressing a close friend, or a person lower in status. The original meaning of *Ohayoo gozaimasu* was "It is early" (with a connotation of respect and politeness); this greeting is therefore most appropriate in the early morning. At 11 A.M., for example, one is more likely to say *Konnichi wa* "Good day!" (see KONNICHI WA).

Unlike "Good morning!", which, on formal occasions, may be used as a farewell in the morning, *Ohayoo gozaimasu* can never be used in parting.

⌐OKAERI-NASAI⌐ お帰りなさい **Welcome home!**

Okaeri-nasai (lit., "You've come home") is the standard
response to *Tadaima* (see TADAIMA). Its closest English
equivalent would be "Welcome home!" or "I'm glad you're
home again," but whereas these English expressions are
reserved for special occasions, *Okaeri-nasai* is a set phrase
used every day.

In rapid, less careful speech, *Okaeri-nasai* regularly becomes *Okaen-nasai*. A higher-status family member speaking
to a lower-status member (e.g., a father speaking to a child)
sometimes shortens the greeting to *Okaeri*.

Okaeri-nasai is also used in non-family situations—for
example, when talking to an in-group person (e.g., to a person working for the same company) who has just returned
from an outing or trip. In this case, *Okaeri-nasai* is never
shortened to *Okaeri*.

OKAGE-SAMA DE おかげさまで **thanks to you**

Okage-sama de, meaning "thanks to you," is often used
even when the person addressed has nothing to do with the
event in question. In (1), a student who has just passed a
college entrance examination is talking to a teacher who
helped him prepare for it; thus the addressee does have a
connection with the happy event. In (2), however, speaker
A has not contributed at all to the good health of B's family.

(1) **Okage-same de pasu-shimashita.**

Thanks to your help, I passed.

(2) A: **Otaku no mina-san ogenki desu ka.**

Is everybody in your family in good health?

B: **Hai, okage-sama de.**

Yes, thank you (lit., thanks to you).

In cases like (2), *Okage-sama de* is like saying "I appreciate your concern" or "Thank you for asking."

As Jorden (1, p. 3) states, *Okage-sama de* "always accompanies, or itself implies, favorable or pleasant information."

OKASHI お菓子 confectionery

Okashi, or its plain form, *kashi,* is a generic term for cake, sweets, and candy whether Japanese or Western. A distinction can be made between Japanese sweet things and Western ones by calling the former *wagashi* (lit., "Japanese *kashi*"), and the latter *yoogashi* (lit., "Western *kashi*").

Wagashi and *yoogashi* can each be divided into subcategories. The most popular type of *wagashi* is *mochigashi* (i.e., *mochi*-based *kashi*) while the most popular type of *yoogashi* is undoubtedly *keeki* "cake [baked Western style]."

OKO-SAN お子さん your child

When you talk about your own child or children, say *kodomo* or *uchi no ko[domo]*, but to refer to a child or children of someone whose status calls for deference in speech, say *oko-san*. Unfortunately *oko-san* sounds very much like *okusan,* meaning "your wife." One has to distinguish them by pronouncing *oko-san* without an accent and *oku-san* by placing an accent on the first syllable, i.e., ōku-san (see OKU-SAN).

(1) **Oko-san wa ogenki desu ka.**
How is your child?

(2) **Oku-san wa ogenki desu ka.**
How is your wife?

OKU-SAN 奥さん **your wife**

Oku-san means "your (*or* someone else's) wife," and contrasts with *kanai,* which refers to the speaker's wife. Until the end of World War II, *oku-san* was used exclusively for the wives of men of average or higher-than-average social status. Women married to men of below-average social status such as merchants and farmers used to be called *oka-mi-san.* After the war, however, *okami-san* came to be thought of as a somewhat discriminatory term. As a result, even wives who would have been called *okami-san* in prewar years are often addressed as *oku-san* nowadays.

OMEDETOO GOZAIMASU おめでとうございます **Congratulations!**

Omedetoo gozaimasu is a very convenient set phrase that may be used to congratulate a person on any happy occasion, be it his birthday, his wedding, or some success he has achieved. *Omedetoo gozaimasu* may be used by itself or together with a word or words referring to a specific occasion.

(1) **Otanjoobi omedetoo gozaimasu.**
Happy birthday!
(2) **Gokekkon omedetoo gozaimasu.**
Congratulations on your wedding!
(3) **Akachan ga oumare ni natte, omedetoo gozaimasu.**
Congratulations on having a new baby!

If the word preceding *omedetoo* is a noun, as in (1) and (2), no particle is used in Japanese that might correspond to "on" in English. If the preceding word is inflected, use the gerund form. In (3), for example, *natte* is the gerund form of *naru.* (See also AKEMASHITE OMEDETOO GOZAIMASU.)

OMOIDASU 思い出す **to bring back from memory**

English "remember" means both (a) "to retain something in the memory" (as in "You should always remember your wife's birthday"), and (b) "to recall" (as in "I suddenly remembered I had some homework"). In Japanese, these two meanings are represented by two different verbs. Meaning (a) is represented by *oboete-iru* (see OBOERU), and meaning (b) by *omoidasu*. In the following examples, therefore, *omoidasu* is correct in (1), but not in (2).

(1) **Shukudai ga aru koto o kyuu ni omoidashita.**
    I suddenly remembered that I had some homework.
(2) **Okusan no otanjoobi wa omoidashita hoo ga ii desu yo.*
    You should remember your wife's birthday.

In sentence (2) above, *omoidashita* should be replaced by *oboete-ita*.

OMOU 思う **to think**

Omou can represent one's judgment, realization, expectation, decision, belief, intention, wish, doubt, etc., but not analytical thinking. It is for this reason that, whereas examples (1) through (3) are correct, (4) and (5) are not.

(1) **Soo omoimasu.** (judgment)
    I think so.
(2) **Ano hito wa kitto kuru to omou.** (belief)
    I think he'll definitely come.
(3) **Kyoo wa hayaku neyoo to omou.** (intention)
    I think I'll go to bed early today.
(4) **Kono mondai o yoku omotte-kudasai.* (analytical thinking)
    Please consider this problem carefully.

(5) *Kare ga naze sonna koto o shita no ka, ikura omotte
     mo wakaranai. (analytical thinking)
     No matter how much I rack my brains, I cannot figure
     out why he did such a thing.

For analytical thinking, *kangaeru* is the verb to be used
(see KANGAERU).

  Omou is used when the object of thinking is mentioned
(or at least clearly implied). *Omou,* therefore, is most commonly preceded by *o* or *to*.

(6) **Ima chotto haha no koto o omotte-iru n desu.**
     I'm just thinking of my mother.

(7) **Watanabe-san wa ii hito da to omou.**
     I think Mr. Watanabe is a very nice person.

ONAJI 同じ the same

Onaji is a noun but behaves much like an adjective (such as
ookii and *chiisai*) in that it can modify a noun without *na*
or *no* in between.

(1) **onaji hito** (not *onaji no hito* or *onaji na hito*)
     the same person

Otherwise it is like any other noun in that it is followed by
ja (or *de wa*) *arimasen* in negative sentences.

(2) **Onaji ja arimasen.**
     It isn't the same.

  This hybrid nature comes from the fact that *onaji* was an
adjective at one time. In fact, its *ku* form is still used in
written Japanese, revealing its origin.

(3) **Iwate-ken wa Aomori-ken to onajiku Toohoku ni ichi-
     shite-iru.**
     Iwate Prefecture, like Aomori Prefecture, is located in
     the Tohoku Region.

ONAKA おなか stomach

The Japanese equivalent of "I am hungry" is normally *Onaka ga suita,* which literally means "My stomach has gotten empty," i.e., "I've become hungry." This interesting difference between the English and the Japanese supports the theory that very often English expressions using stative verbs correspond to Japanese expressions using verbs that basically mean "to become such-and-such" or "to do such-and-such" (Kunihiro, pp. 88–89). Other examples are:

(1) **Nodo ga kawaita.**
I am thirsty. (lit., My throat has gotten dry.)

(2) **Kinoo kekkon-shita.**
He was married yesterday. (lit., He married yesterday.)

(3) **Ima sugu ikimasu.**
I'll be there in a minute. (lit., I'll go in a minute.)

(4) **Ashita itsutsu ni naru.**
He will be five tomorrow. (lit., He'll become five tomorrow.)

(5) **Fuyu ga owatta.**
Winter is over. (lit., Winter has ended.)

(6) **Haru ga kita.**
Spring is here. (lit., Spring has come.)

(7) **Shinda.**
He is dead. (lit., He has died.)

Another version of *Onaka ga suita* is *Hara ga hetta,* which also means "I'm hungry." Although usually explained as a vulgar expression, *Hara ga hetta* is acceptable if used by men among close friends and associates on informal occasions.

ONEGAI-SHIMASU お願いします lit., I [humbly] request

Onegai-shimasu is the humble form of the verb *negau* meaning "to request," and is used very often in all sorts of request-making situations. For example, when one goes into a store and doesn't see the shopkeeper or any salesclerk, one can call out *Onegai-shimasu!* meaning "Hello!" (lit., "I [humbly] request [your service]"). Even if you see someone working for the store, you can still say *Onegai-shimasu* to attract his attention.

You can say *Onegai-shimasu* also when you ask for specific items of your choice at a store, a restaurant, etc.

(1) **Kono ringo o mittsu onegai-shimasu.**

I'd like three of these apples, please. (lit., I [humbly] request three of these apples.)

(2) **Sukiyaki o onegai-shimasu.**

I'd like sukiyaki. (lit., I [humbly] request sukiyaki.)

In the examples above, *onegai-shimasu* may be replaced by *kudasai* (lit., "please give me") without causing any change in meaning, the only difference being that the *onegai-shimasu* versions are a little more polite.

During election campaigns, all candidates shout out *Onegai-shimasu!* repeatedly instead of calmly discussing relevant issues. With *Onegai-shimasu!* and humble bows, they are of course soliciting votes from their constituents.

When one entrusts something to someone else, e.g., "when submitting papers such as application forms . . . in a government office, bank, and the like" (Mizutani and Mizutani, 1, p. 59), one often says

(3) **Kore o onegai-shimasu.**

Please take care of this for me. (lit., I request this.)

Suppose you go to see someone with a request. You present him with the request, he says, "All right," and you engage in small talk briefly. Now, what would you say to conclude the conversation? The best thing to say would be

(4) **Ja onegai-shimasu.**

Well then, please take care of it for me.

What you are really saying is "I ask that you kindly comply with the request I have just made." This parting remark serves as an act of confirmation.

⌐ ¬
ONNA 女 female

Onna "female" corresponds to *otoko* "male" (see OTOKO). *Onna* corresponds to *otoko, onna-no-ko* "girl" to *otoko-no-ko* "boy," *onna-no-hito* "woman" to *otoko-no-hito* "man," and *onna-no-kata* "lady" to *otoko-no-kata* "gentleman."

In somewhat vulgar Japanese, *onna* sometimes means "paramour," as in *kare no onna* "his woman."

¬
OOI 多い many, much

Ooi means "a lot," in terms of both numbers and quantities.
(1) **Konogoro wa ame ga ooi.** (quantity)
    It's been raining a lot lately.
(2) **Nyuuyooku ni wa kokujin ga ooi.** (number)
    In New York, there are many blacks.

⌐ ¬
OOKII 大きい big, large

Ookii often becomes *ooki na* (not **ookii na*) when placed before a noun.
(1) **ookii** (or **ooki na**) **hon**
    a big book
Shibata, 1970 (pp. 20–21), states that Tokyoites feel more comfortable with *na* while Osakaites are more likely to use -*i* than *na*. Morita (p. 118), on the other hand, distinguishes *ookii* from *ooki na,* saying that *ookii* is for concrete objects

and *ooki na* for abstract nouns, citing such examples as

(2) **ookii ie (hito, machi,** etc.)
a big house (person, town, etc.)

(3) **ooki na jiken (seikoo, shippai,** etc.)
a big event (success, failure, etc.)

It is quite doubtful, however, how many speakers of Japanese really observe these distinctions. It is my guess that to most Japanese *ookii* and *ooki na* are simply interchangeable.

Ooki na is like one word in that *ooki* and *na* are inseparable. Although *ooki* is listed as a *na*-noun by Jorden (2, p. 368), it is quite different from other *na*-nouns such as *kirei* "pretty, clean" (see KIREI). *Kirei,* for example, can be used without a following *na,* as in

(5) **Kirei desu nee.**
Isn't it pretty!

(6) **Heya o kirei ni shite-kudasai.**
Please tidy up your room.

Ooki, on the other hand, can never be used without *na* + following noun.

With regard to a voice, one hardly ever uses "a big voice" in English to mean "a loud voice." In Japanese, *ookii* (or *ooki na*) *koe* "a loud voice" (lit., "a big voice") is a common expression. Similarly, "to make the sound [of a TV, radio, etc.] louder" is *ookiku suru* (lit., "to make big").

(7) **Rajio ga kikoenai kara, motto ookiku shite.**
I can't hear the radio very well. Will you turn it up?
(lit., Will you make it bigger?)

ORIRU 降りる，下りる **to go down, to get off**

Oriru meaning "to go down" takes the particle *o* when the place where the act of going down takes place is mentioned as in

(1) **kaidan (yama, saka,** etc.) **o oriru**
  to go down the stairs (mountain, slope, etc.)

This is also true of *oriru* meaning "to get off, to get out of [a vehicle]."

(2) (a) **basu** (or **densha**) **o oriru**
    to get off the bus (*or* train)

  (b) **kuruma** (or **takushii**) **o oriru**
    to get out of the car (*or* taxi)

In example (2) above, *kara* "from, out of" could be used instead of *o,* but *o* is more common.

OSHIERU 教える to teach, to tell, to inform

Oshieru basically means "to impart [something, e.g., information, to someone]." Although it is often equated with "teach," it does not always correspond to that.

(1) **kodomo ni suugaku o oshieru**
  to teach children mathematics

(2) **hito ni eki e iku michi o oshieru**
  to tell a person the way to the station

(3) **hito ni kikai no tsukaikata o oshieru**
  to show a person how to use a machine

When the idea of "to someone" is expressed, the particle *ni* is used as in the three examples above. When *oshieru* is used in the sense of "teach" (and not "tell" or "show"), however, the person being taught might become the direct object with the attachment of *o* instead of *ni.*

(4) **Kodomo o oshieru no wa muzukashii.**
  It is difficult to teach children.

In this case, the subject being taught becomes irrelevant.

OSOI 遅い slow, late

Osoi means both "slow" and "late." This probably indicates that, in the Japanese speaker's mind, slowness and lateness are closely connected. After all, if you travel slowly, you get to your destination late!

Sometimes, *osoi* might cause ambiguity as in the case of *osoi kisha,* which can mean either "a late train" or "a slow train," but usually this kind of ambiguity disappears with sufficient contextual information, as in

(1) **Asa roku-ji shuppatsu ja haya-sugiru n desu ga, motto osoi kisha wa arimasen ka.**

Leaving at six in the morning would be too early. Aren't there later trains?

However, *osoku,* the adverbial form of *osoi,* only means "late," and not "slowly" (Morita, p. 130).

(2) **Kesa wa osoku okimashita.**

This morning I got up late.

To express the meaning of "slowly," use *yukkuri* (see YUKKURI).

(3) **Motto yukkuri** (not **osoku*) **tabeta hoo ga ii desu yo.**

You should eat more slowly.

OTAKU お宅 your home

While *taku* meaning "my home" or "my husband" is not used very often, its honorific counterpart *otaku* is used all the time to refer to the house of someone (most often the addressee) whom the speaker wishes to treat with deference.

(1) **Uchida-sensei no otaku no denwa-bangoo wa nan-ban deshoo ka.**

What's Professor Uchida's home phone number?

(2) **Ashita no ban chotto otaku ni ukagatte mo yoroshii desu ka.**

May I visit your house for a little while tomorrow evening?

(3) **Are wa otaku no obotchan desu ka.**

Is that your son? (lit., Is that the son of your home?)

In recent years, *otaku* has come to be used increasingly more frequently as the politer version of *anata* "you," as in

(4) **Otaku wa dochira ni osumai desu ka.**

Where do you live?

OTETSUDAI-SAN お手伝いさん [house]maid

Until the end of World War II, *jochuu* was the standard term for "housemaid." After the war, however, with the influx of a new democratic spirit, the Japanese people began to interpret the word as a derogatory term referring to the exploited class of housemaids. A new word, *otetsudai-san* (lit., "helper"), came into being as a result. Even with this respectable title, housemaids are hard to come by. Young girls from rural areas, who would have gladly become housemaids in urban areas in prewar Japan, would rather seek jobs at factories and offices now, where they can enjoy more freedom and better benefits.

In connection with this, the way maids are addressed has also improved. Until the end of World War II, a maid with the first name *Haruko,* for example, was often not even *Haruko*. -*Ko* was deleted, and instead the prefix *o-* was attached to the name, forming *Oharu,* and giving the name a rather old-fashioned flavor. Nowadays, not only are maids never given this prefix, but they are always addressed more respectfully with -*san* added (e.g., *Haruko-san*).

Otetsudai-san, however, is still considered a newly coined term, and its usage has not become completely established. For example, how does a maid refer to her occupation? Can she call herself *otetsudai-san,* or should she just call herself *otetsudai?* Should one refer to one's maid as *otetsudai* or *otetsudai-san* when one talks to outsiders? Usage varies on these points.

OTOKO 男 male

Otoko "male" by itself is a plain term and often carries a derogatory tone when used in reference to a specific person, especially in speech (though generally not in written Japanese). *Otoko-no-hito* "man" has no such connotation.

(1) **Ano otoko wa iya na yatsu da na.**
   Isn't that guy nasty?

(2) **Ano otoko-no-hito wa shinsetsu desu nee**?
   Isn't that man kind?

In sentence (1), *otoko* is more appropriate than *otoko-no-hito* because of *iya na yatsu* "a nasty guy," which carries a negative value. In (2), on the other hand, *otoko* would sound a little strange unless the speaker wished to convey the idea that he himself is decidedly of higher status than the man he is talking about.

To make *otoko-no-hito* even more polite, *otoko-no-kata* "gentleman" should be used.

(3) **Ano otoko-no-kata wa donata deshoo ka.**
   Who could that gentleman be?

In English, "man" sometimes means "human being," as in "Man is mortal." *Otoko* (and *otoko-no-hito*) cannot be so used. *Ningen* is the word for that.

In somewhat vulgar Japanese, *otoko* sometimes means "lover," as in

(4) **Toshiko wa otoko ni suterareta.**
    Toshiko was left by her lover.

┌   ┐
OTOOTO 弟 **younger brother**

In Japanese, there is no genuine equivalent of "brother."
While in English one can talk about one's brother without
indicating who is older, in Japanese one generally talks
about one's *ani* "older brother" (see ANI) or *otooto* "younger
brother."

Otooto, first of all, means "younger brothers in general."

(1) **Nihon de wa otooto wa ani no meshita da.**
    In Japan, younger brothers are of lower status than
    older brothers.

Second, *otooto* refers to one's own younger brother when
one is talking to an outsider.

(2) **Otooto ga yatto Toodai ni hairimashita.**
    My younger brother has finally gotten into Tokyo Uni-
    versity.

When talking to someone about his brother, use *otootosan.*

(3) **Otooto-san ga Toodai ni ohairi ni natta soo desu ne.**
    I hear your younger brother has gotten into Tokyo
    University.

When talking to someone about a third person's brother,
use *otooto-san* (though *otooto* is also possible if, for example,
you are talking to a member of your family about the younger brother of a close friend of yours).

(4) **Yamanaka-san no otooto-san wa ima Amerika-ryuuga-
    ku-chuu desu.**
    Mr. Yamanaka's younger brother is studying in Amer-
    ica now.

An older brother or an older sister addresses his/her
younger brother not as *otooto* but by his given name.

(5) **Saburoo,** | (a) **gohan da yo.** (an older brother speaking) |
 | (b) **gohan yo.** (an older sister speaking) |
Saburo, it's dinner time!

OTSURI おつり change

Otsuri corresponds to "change" in a limited way.

(1) **Sen-en-satsu o dashitara, nihyaku-en otsuri ga kita.**
I gave them a 1,000-yen bill and received 200 yen in change.

"Change" can also refer to money given in exchange for an equivalent of higher denomination. For example, if you wish to exchange a 1,000-yen bill for the same amount in coins, you can say in English

(2) I need change for a 1,000-yen bill.

This kind of change is not *otsuri*. The Japanese equivalent of (2) would be

(3) **Sen-en-satsu o komakaku shi-tai n desu ga.**
lit., I'd like to make a 1,000-yen bill smaller.

"Change" can also mean "small coins," as in

(4) I always carry some change in my pants pocket.

This kind of change is not *otsuri,* but *kozeni* (lit., "small money").

In short, "change" is much broader in meaning than *otsuri*. *Otsuri* may be used only in reference to a balance of money returned at the time of purchase.

OWARU 終わる to end

Owaru can be either transitive, as in (1), or intransitive, as in (2).

(1) **Kurasu ga owatta.** (intransitive)
    The class ended.
(2) **Kurasu o owatta.** (transitive)
    I ended the class.

Owaru has, however, a transitive counterpart, *oeru,* which cannot be used intransitively.

(3) **Kurasu o oeta.**
    I ended the class.

Although to me, (2) and (3) have no difference in meaning except that (3) may sound a little more bookish than (2), *oeru* connotes, according to Morita (p. 386), "consciously ending something."

OYASUMI-NASAI お休みなさい Good night!

Oyasumi-nasai is a farewell one directs to a person who is already in bed or is about to go to bed. It is therefore most commonly heard late in the evening. For example, you say *Oyasumi-nasai* at the time of leaving someone's home after spending an evening there. Unlike English "Good night!", *Oyasumi-nasai* may not be used as one leaves the office at 5 P.M. That would be too early for *Oyasumi-nasai,* which literally means "Sleep well!"

OYU お湯 hot water

Oyu (or the less often used plain form *yu*) means "hot water." In English, "water" may be hot or cold. In Japanese, on the other hand, water is called either *mizu* "cold water" (see MIZU) or *oyu,* depending on its temperature. Although *oyu* by itself (i.e., without an accompanying modifier) can refer to hot water, to mean "really hot water," it is perfectly correct and not redundant to say

(1) **atsui oyu**
    really hot water

Sometimes, *oyu* is used in place of *ofuro* (see OFURO) to mean "bath" (but not "bathtub").

RIKAI-SURU 理解する **to comprehend**

Rikai-suru meaning "to comprehend" is a transitive verb. Unlike *wakaru,* which takes *ga,* it therefore takes *o.*

(1) **Nihonjin wa Nihon o rikai-suru gaikokujin wa amari inai to omotte-iru.**
    The Japanese feel that there are few foreigners who understand Japan.

Another difference is that while *wakaru* is an everyday expression, *rikai-suru* is a written form.

While *wakaru* does not represent a controllable action and cannot therefore take a potential form *(*wakareru), rikai-suru* is considered to represent a controllable action and can take a potential form, i.e., *rikai-dekiru.*

(2) **Konna yasashii koto de mo rikai-dekinai** (not **wakarenai**) **hito ga iru rashii.**
    There are apparently some people who cannot even understand such a simple thing as this.

(See also WAKARU.)

RUSU 留守 **not at home**

Rusu should not be explained as "out," "away," or "absent," but more specifically as "not at home."

(1) **Kinoo Tomita-san no uchi ni denwa o shimashita ga rusu deshita.**

I called Mr. Tomita's home yesterday but he was not at home.

(2) **Sekkaku yotte-kudasatta no ni rusu o shite, shitsurei shimashita.**

I'm sorry I wasn't home when you kindly stopped by my house.

The following example is a dialogue once written by a student of mine who identified *rusu* with "absent."

(3) A: **Nakamura-san wa kinoo kaisha ni kimashita ka.**

Did Mr. Nakamura come to work yesterday?

B: **Iie, rusu deshita.*

No, he was absent.

To express the idea of "No, he was absent," this student should have written one of the following alternatives:

(4) (a) **Iie, kimasen deshita.**

No, he didn't come.

(b) **Iie, yasumi deshita.**

No, he was absent.

(c) **Iie, kekkin-shimashita.**

No, he missed work.

RYOKOO-SURU 旅行する **to travel**

Ryokoo-suru refers to traveling done by humans. In English, it is possible to say, for example, "Light travels faster than sound"; in Japanese, on the other hand, one would have to use an entirely different expression and say *Hikari no sokudo wa oto no sokudo yori hayai* "The speed of light is faster than that of sound."

"Travel" basically means "to move (*or* go) from place to

place"; therefore it can even refer to daily commuting, as in "I have to travel quite a distance to get to my office every day." *Ryokoo-suru,* on the other hand, implies a specially planned trip for business or for pleasure, and cannot be used for daily commuting.

SAKAYA 酒屋 saké store

A *sakaya* is a saké store, but it sells other kinds of liquor such as beer and whiskey as well. It is quite different from an American liquor store, however. At a *sakaya,* liquor is only one of the many items sold. The majority of the merchandise is groceries such as sugar, canned food, and *miso* "soy-bean paste."

Sakaya should not be confused with *sakaba,* a kind of bar.

SAKE 酒 saké, liquor

Sake (or, more politely, *osake*) can refer to either (a) Japanese rice wine, or (b) alcoholic beverages generally. In (1) below, *sake* is used with meaning (a), while in (2) it has meaning (b).
(1) **Osake wa arimasen ga biiru wa arimasu.**
    We don't have saké, but we have beer.
(2) **Ano hito wa sake mo tabako mo nomimasen.**
    He neither drinks liquor nor smokes.
   To avoid this confusion, however, *nihonshu* "Japanese rice wine" is sometimes used for meaning (a), and *arukooru* (lit., "alcohol") for meaning (b), as in
(3) **Kyoo wa nihonshu ni shimashoo.**
    Let's have saké today.

(4) **Ano hito wa arukooru ni tsuyoi desu nee.**
He can certainly hold his liquor, can't he!

SAKKA 作家 **writer, novelist**

A *sakka* is a fiction writer and most commonly a novelist. The word is used with reference to a person's occupation as a writer (or novelist).

(1) **Kawabata wa Nihon no daihyoo-teki na sakka datta.**
Kawabata was a representative writer (*or* novelist) of Japan.

Sakka cannot be used with regard to the authorship of a specific book. In (2) below, *sakka* is wrong; it has to be replaced by *sakusha* "the author of a specific work of fiction."

(2) **Kono shoosetsu no sakusha** (not **sakka*) **wa Mishima desu.**
The author of this novel is Mishima.

(See also CHOSHA and SHOOSETSUKA.)

SAMUI 寒い **cold**

Samui "cold" represents a sensation of coldness perceived throughout the whole body.

(1) **Kyoo wa samui.**
It's cold today.

Samui is never used in reference to solids or fluids. Examples (2) and (3) below are therefore incorrect.

(2) **samui te*
lit., cold hand

(3) **samui juusu*
lit., cold juice

In such cases, *samui* has to be replaced by *tsumetai* (see TSUMETAI).

Some nouns may be modified by either *samui* or *tsumetai*.
(4) (a) **samui kaze**
     cold wind
    (b) **tsumetai kaze**
     cold wind

There is, however, a slight difference between (4a) and (4b). (4a) represents the cold wind as something affecting one's whole body, whereas (4b) represents the coldness of the wind as it affects one's skin, one's face, or one's hands only.

-SAN さん (suffix attached to a name)

-San most commonly follows a person's family name (or family name plus given name) to function somewhat like "Mr.," "Mrs.," or "Miss," as in *Tanaka-san* or *Tanaka Ichiroo-san*. Unlike "Mr.," "Mrs.," and "Miss," however, *-san* is not used when addressing a person higher in status than the speaker. For example, a company employee speaking to his boss does not use *-san* but rather uses the latter's title as a term of address, e.g., *shachoo* "company president," *buchoo* "department chief," or *kachoo* "section chief." A student speaking to his teacher does not as a rule use *-san* either but calls him *sensei* (see SENSEI) instead.

-San may also be attached to given names alone. This is the case when one addresses cousins, maids, neighbors' children, etc. (e.g., *Taroo-san, Michiko-san*). *-San* may be added to occupation names to address, or refer to, people in certain occupations. Carpenters, gardeners, bakers, for example, are often called *daiku-san* (lit., "Mr. Carpenter"),

uekiya-san (lit., "Mr. Gardener"), and *pan'ya-san* (lit., "Mr. Baker"), respectively. *-San* is also used with kinship terms in addressing one's relatives if the addressee is higher in status than the speaker, e.g., *otoo-san* "father," *okaa-san* "mother," *oji-san* "uncle," and *oba-san* "aunt." When one addresses one's own children, grandchildren, or younger siblings, one uses their names without *-san,* although *-chan* (the diminutive variant of *-san*) may sometimes be used.

-San is never used by itself, nor is it ever used in reference to oneself.

SANPO 散歩 walk, stroll

Sanpo is a noun meaning "a walk" or "a stroll," and *sanpo-suru* is the corresponding compound verb meaning "to take a walk (*or* stroll)." *Sanpo* only refers to a leisurely walk for exercise or for pleasure, and should not be used when a specific destination is mentioned or when some business is involved. If one walks to the office, for example, it is not a *sanpo.*

(1) **Maiasa kaisha made sanpo-shimasu.*

I take a walk to the office every day.

This sentence has to be rephrased, for example, like the following:

(2) **Maiasa kaisha made aruite ikimasu.**

I walk to the office every day.

SAYONARA さよなら Good-by

Sayonara (or, more formally, *Sayoonara*) is the most common farewell that may be used at any time of the day.

However, it carries a rather informal tone and therefore does not go well with *keigo* (respect language). An adult is unlikely to say *Sayonara* or *Sayoonara* to a person of much higher status. For example, an employee would normally use *Shitsurei-shimasu* (lit., "Excuse me [for leaving]") as he parts with his boss.

Sayonara is not appropriate for all occasions of leave-taking. For example, it cannot be used when one leaves one's own home (*Itte-mairimasu* is the correct expression then), or when one sees off a member of one's own household (*Itte-irasshai* is the set phrase for that occasion) (see ITTE-MAIRIMASU and ITTE-IRASSHAI).

SEIFU 政府 government

In English, "government" may refer to any level of government. You can talk about a city government, a state government, or a federal government. In Japanese, on the other hand, *seifu* is generally reserved for a national government only. It is therefore correct to say *Nihon-seifu* "the Japanese government" or *Amerika-seifu* "the American government," but not, for example, **ken-seifu* (lit., "prefectural government"). *Kenchoo* "prefectural office" is used instead.

SEITO 生徒 student, pupil

In English, a person attending almost any kind of school from elementary school to college and beyond may be called a student. In Japanese, on the other hand, *gakusei* (see GAKUSEI) and *seito,* both meaning "student," are fairly clearly distinguished from each other, the former being reserved mostly for college and university students, and the latter for younger students in nursery school through high school. The line of demarcation is somewhat blurred, however, high school students sometimes being referred to as *gakusei*.

Students taking private lessons are not *gakusei* but *seito* regardless of age. For example, a housewife taking piano lessons from a tutor is his *seito*. Note the difference between the two words.

(1) **Ano piano no sensei ni wa seito ga takusan aru. Gakusei mo, shufu mo, komodo mo iru.**

That piano teacher has lots of private students—[college] students, housewives, and children.

SEMAI 狭い **narrow, small in area**

Semai is the opposite of *hiroi* "wide" (see HIROI). As is the case with *hiroi, semai* is used both one-dimensionally as in sentence (1), and two-dimensionally as in (2).

(1) **semai michi (mon, toguchi,** etc.)

narrow road (gate, doorway, etc.)

(2) **semai heya (niwa, kuni,** etc.)

small (i.e., limited in space) room (yard, country, etc.)

When used two-dimensionally, *semai* is similar in meaning to *chiisai* "small," but these two adjectives are different in focus. *Chiisai* is simply "small in size," whereas *semai* signifies "not spacious enough for a particular purpose." Even a *chiisai* room may not be *semai* if occupied by someone without furniture, while even an *ookii* "large" room could become *semai* if used for a huge banquet (Suzuki, p. 80). One might say that *semai* carries a negative connotation while *chiisai* doesn't.

SENJITSU 先日 the other day

Senjitsu is probably used most often in greetings such as
(1) **Senjitsu wa gochisoo-sama deshita.**
Thank you for the treat the other day.
(2) **Senjitsu wa doomo arigatoo gozaimashita.**
Thank you for what you did for me the other day.

In Japan, when two people meet after a few days (perhaps up to a week or two), each tries to remember in words what favor the other person did for him the last time they met. Even if the other person might not have done any favor at all, one often acknowledges the last meeting by saying something less specific such as
(3) **Senjitsu wa doomo shitsurei-shimashita.**
lit., I was rude the other day.
This expression is used even when the speaker did nothing rude at all. It is merely the Japanese way of saying "It was good to see you (*or* talk to you) the other day." In fact, (3) is a good example of how Japanese speakers have a tendency to apologize where English speakers would express happiness or pleasure (e.g., "It was good to see you," "I enjoyed talking to you," "Your party was simply great," etc.).

If one wishes to be even less specific than (3) above one can simply say
(4) **Senjitsu wa doomo.**
This could be an abbreviation of either (2) or (3). Precisely because of its vagueness, this expression is considered very convenient and is used quite frequently.

Senjitsu is a formal expression and should be replaced by *kono-aida* in informal speech (see KONO-AIDA).

SENPAI 先輩 lit., one's senior

If a person enters, and graduates from, the same school or

college that you do, but ahead of you in time, even by one year, he is a *senpai* to you, and you don't refer to him as a *tomodachi* "friend" (see TOMODACHI). Men observe these terminology rules much more rigidly than women do. Suppose Tanaka and Suzuki, both men, graduated from the same high school or college, with Tanaka graduating a year or two before Suzuki. If they meet, Tanaka will call Suzuki either *Suzuki* or *Suzuki-kun,* but Suzuki will address Tanaka as *Tanaka-san.* (In this particular instance, women's speech might be called more democratic than men's. If Tanaka and Suzuki above were both women, they would call each other *Tanaka-san* and *Suzuki-san.*)

Being a *senpai* thus gives one higher status in Japanese human relations, but at the same time this is accompanied by "noblesse oblige." It is tacitly understood in Japanese society that *senpai* are supposed to look after the well-being of their *koohai* "juniors," especially if they used to belong to the same athletic team in school or college. In fact, high-school or college athletic teams in Japan are often coached by *senpai* who volunteer their service free of charge. (See also KOOHAI.)

SENSEI 先生 teacher

Sensei has two uses. First of all, it means "teacher."
(1) **Ano hito wa kookoo no sensei da soo da.**
     I hear he is a high-school teacher.
Second, it is used as a respectful term of address for people in certain professions, e.g., teachers, doctors, dentists, writers, lawyers, and politicians.
(2) **Sensei, ashita wa gotsugoo ga yoroshii deshoo ka.**
     Would tomorrow be convenient for you?
This second use of *sensei* is impossible to translate into

English because there is no equivalent. (It is for this reason that the translator of Soseki Natsume's novel *Kokoro* used the Japanese word *sensei* throughout the English version for the elderly gentleman who is called *sensei* and otherwise remains nameless in the original.) In situations such as (2) above, the English speaker would use the name of the addressee, e.g., "Dr. (*or* Mr., Mrs., Miss) Miller, would tomorrow be convenient for you?"

There is another word, *kyooshi*, which also means "teacher," but there are several differences between this word and *sensei*. First of all, *kyooshi* does not refer to anyone but teachers. Second, it is never used as a term of address. Third, the word *sensei* carries with it a connotation of respect and is therefore not used in reference to oneself. When a teacher mentions his occupation to someone else, he should say, for example,

(3) **Kookoo no kyooshi** (not **sensei*) **o shite-imasu.**
    I am a high-school teacher.

Fourth, except when one is referring to oneself, *kyooshi* is mostly a written form. It is not a conversational expression like *sensei* and is rarely used by children.

SENTAKU 洗濯 washing

Sentaku means "washing, laundering," and it becomes a compound verb with the addition of *suru*, i.e., *sentaku-suru*, meaning "to wash, to launder." *Sentaku* refers only to washing clothes, linens, etc., and is, in this sense, quite different from *arau* "to wash," which may refer to washing anything. In sentence (1), therefore, either *sentaku-suru* or *arau* would be all right, but in (2), *arau* would be the only correct verb.

(1) **Ato de kutsushita o sentaku-suru** (or **arau**) **tsumori desu.**
I plan to wash some socks later.

(2) **Te o arai-nasai** (not *_sentaku-shi-nasai_).
Wash your hands.

English "wash" does not always require an object. For example, in "Monday is the day we wash," "wash" by itself means "wash clothes" and doesn't need an object. In Japanese, on the other hand, although _sentaku-suru_ does not always need an object, _arau_ does. In the following example, therefore, only (a) would be correct.

(3) **Getsuyoo ga** | (a) **sentaku-bi** | **desu.**
⎪ (b) *_arau hi_ |
Monday is our wash day.

SHIBAI 芝居 play

Shibai means "play" in the sense of "theatrical performance" or "show."

(1) **Kyoo wa shibai o mi ni ikimashoo.**
Let's go and see a play today.

(2) **Are wa ii shibai deshita yo.**
That was a good play.

Shibai may also mean "playacting, putting on an act."

(3) **Hontoo ni naite-iru n ja arimasen. Shibai desu yo.**
She isn't really crying. She's just faking it.

Dramas one reads are usually not _shibai,_ but _gikyoku_ (although when a _gikyoku_ is performed on stage, it is referred to as a _shibai_).

(4) **Chehofu no gikyoku** (not *_shibai_) **wa zuibun yonda ga, shibai wa mada mita koto ga nai.**
I've read a lot of dramas by Chekhov but I've never seen any of them performed.

"Drama" in the sense of "theater arts" is not *shibai,* but *engeki.*

(5) **Ano hito wa daigaku de engeki o senkoo-shite-imasu.**
He is majoring in theater arts in college.

An amateur play staged by young students, especially elementary-school children, is usually called *geki* rather than *shibai.*

(6) **Uchi no ko wa kondo gakugeikai de geki ni deru soo desu.**
Our child says he'll be in a play at the school's art festival.

When *geki* is used in compounds, however, there is no connotation of amateurishness. For example, *kageki* "opera," *shuukyoogeki* "religious play," etc., just represent different categories of plays.

Plays written and produced for radio or TV are called *dorama* (from English "drama")—more specifically, *rajio-dorama* (lit., "radio drama") or *terebi-dorama* (lit., "TV drama").

SHIKAKU 四角 square

Shikaku literally means "four-cornered [shape]." It follows, therefore, that the word may refer not only to squares but to rectangular shapes as well. When one has to make a distinction between the two, one may say *seihookei* for "a square" and *choohookei* for "a rectangular shape."

SHIKEN 試験 examination

Don't translate "take an examination" directly into Japanese and say *shiken o toru (lit., "to take an examination"). The correct expression is *shiken o ukeru* (lit., "to receive an examination").

(1) **Miyata-kun wa Toodai no nyuugaku-shiken o ukeru soo da.**

I hear Miyata will be taking the entrance examination for Tokyo University.

Unlike English "examination," *shiken* does not normally refer to examination papers. A sheet of paper with examination questions is called *shiken-mondai* before the answers are written in, and *tooan* (lit., "answer draft") afterward.

(2) Teacher: **Ima shiken-mondai** (not **shiken*) **o tsukutte-iru n desu.**

I'm preparing an exam.

(3) Teacher (after exams): **Tooan** (not **shiken*) **o takusan shirabenakucha naranai n desu.**

I've got to read lots of exams.

SHIRU 知る to get to know

Shiru is a very strange verb. To express the idea of "I don't know," we use the nonpast negative, as in

(1) **Shirimasen.** (or **Shiranai.**)

I don't know.

However, to express the idea of "I know," we must use the *-te-iru* form, as in

(2) **Shitte-imasu.** (or **Shitte-iru.**)

I know. (lit., I am in the state of having gotten to know.)

In other words, for some reason, we never use *Shirimasu* (or *Shiru*) to mean "I know," nor do we usually use *Shitte-imasen* (or *Shitte-inai*) to mean "I don't know." (Although we occasionally hear *Shitte-imasen* or *Shitte-inai,* they are not common expressions.) The reason "I know" is *Shitte-iru* is because *shiru* is a punctual verb meaning "to get to know," and not a stative verb meaning "to know." *Shitte-iru,* therefore, literally means "I am in the state of having gotten to know." The question still remains, however, why *Shitte-inai* (lit., "I am not in the state of having gotten to know") is not as common an expression as *Shiranai* in the sense of "I don't know." No other verb behaves quite like this.

English "I don't know" does not always correspond to *Shirimasen* (or *Shiranai*) in Japanese; it sometimes corresponds to *Wakarimasen* (or *Wakaranai*). For the difference between these two Japanese expressions, see WAKARU.

SHITAMACHI 下町 downtown

Shitamachi literally means "lower town" and refers mostly to the low-lying areas of Tokyo, such as Asakusa, Kanda, and Shiba, where, during the Edo period, the townspeople (mainly merchants) resided. This is the home of genuine *Edokko* "Edoites," the speakers of *shitamachi* speech, which is known for its lack of distinction between *hi* and *shi*. (Incidentally, in the Japanese version of *My Fair Lady,* Eliza Doolittle speaks this sort of *shitamachi* speech as the Japanese equivalent of Cockney.)

To equate *shitamachi* with English "downtown" is absolutely erroneous. For one thing, any good-sized town has a downtown section, whereas *shitamachi* is used almost exclusively in reference to Tokyo. For another, *shitamachi* is not as frequently used in Japanese as "downtown" is in English. The English speaker always is talking about going downtown, eating downtown, or shopping downtown. That is all part of everyday language. The Japanese counterparts of these expressions, however, do not ordinarily contain the word *shitamachi*. Even in Tokyo, which has a section called *shitamachi,* one does not use, for example, **Kyoo wa shitamachi e ikimashoo* to mean "Let's go downtown today." Instead, one would refer to specific sections of Tokyo, as in *Kyoo wa Ginza e ikimashoo* "Let's go to the Ginza today," *Kyoo wa Shinjuku de eiga o mimashita* "I saw a movie in Shinjuku today," or *Shibuya de shokuji o shimashita* "I ate [at a restaurant] in Shibuya." The word *shitamachi* is used primarily to describe a person's background, as in *Ano hito wa shitamachi-sodachi desu yo* "He grew up in *shitamachi.*"

SHITSUREI-SHIMASU 失礼します **Excuse me**

Shitsurei-shimasu and *Shitsurei-shimashita* both become "Excuse me" in English, but they should be clearly distinguished. *Shitsurei-shimasu* means "I am going to commit an act of rudeness" while *Shitsurei-shimashita* means "I have committed an act of rudeness." The former, therefore, should be used to mean "Excuse me" for something you are about to do—for example, before going into your teacher's office. The latter, on the other hand, should be used to mean "Excuse me" for something you have already done, such as having bothered the addressee.

Shitsurei-shimasu and *Shitsurei-shimashita* are also used in situations that English speakers do not normally consider worth apologizing for. For example, Japanese say *Shitsurei-shimasu* when invited into someone's home. We regularly say *Shitsurei-shimasu* as a farewell instead of *Sayonara* when parting with someone higher in status than we are. It is normal for us to say *Senjitsu wa shitsurei-shimashita* when we see someone with whom we have done something recently, e.g., dining out together. The English equivalent in such a case would not be "I'm sorry for what I did the other day," but rather "It was good to see you the other day."

In informal conversation, both *Shitsurei-shimasu* and *Shitsurei-shimashita* become *Shitsurei*.

SHOOSETSU 小説 novel, short story

A *shoosetsu* is a work of fiction, be it a novel or a short story. In other words, the Japanese language does not generally make a distinction between novels and short stories. When it is necessary to do so, however, one can use the term *choohen-shoosetsu* (lit., "long *shoosetsu*") for novels and *tanpen-shoosetsu* (lit., "short *shoosetsu*") for short stories.

SHOOSETSUKA 小説家 novelist

Shoosetsuka means "novelist" or "writer of short stories." Thus it has a narrower range of meaning than *sakka,* which, although it most often means "novelist," can also refer to playwrights (see SAKKA, also CHOSHA).

SHOOTAI-SURU 招待する to invite

Shootai-suru "to invite" is a formal expression and is usually used with expressions denoting formal affairs.

(1) **hito o kekkonshiki (en'yuukai, kaiten-iwai,** etc.) **ni shootai-suru**
    to invite a person to a wedding (a garden party, the opening of a store, etc.)

In daily conversation, especially in reference to less formal affairs, *yobu* is the verb used.

(2) **Kinoo wa Ishida-san no uchi e yuushoku ni yobareta n desu.**

Yesterday I was invited to dinner at the Ishidas.

Yobu implies that the person invited comes to where the inviter is. On the other hand, if you wish to ask someone to go somewhere with you, use *sasou* to mean "Let's go to such-and-such a place."

(3) **tomodachi o eiga (shibai, ongakukai, etc.) ni sasou**

to ask a friend out to a movie (play, concert, etc.)

SOO DESU そうです That's right

Soo desu meaning "That is so" and its negative counterpart *Soo ja arimasen* meaning "That isn't so" are most normally used in response to a question that ends with a noun + *desu ka* (or *ja arimasen ka*).

(1) A: **Are wa Tanaka-san desu ka.**

Is that Mr. Tanaka?

B: **Hai, soo desu.**

Yes, it is.

(2) A: **Are wa Suzuki-san desu ka.**

Is that Mr. Suzuki?

B: **Iie, soo ja arimasen. Tanaka-san desu yo.**

No, it isn't. It's Mr. Tanaka.

In response to a question that ends with an adjective + *desu ka* or a verb + *ka*, don't use *Soo desu*, but repeat the same adjective or verb instead.

(3) A: **Sore wa oishii desu ka.**

Is that delicious?

B: **Ee, oishii desu yo.**

Yes, it is [delicious].

(4) A: **Takano-san wa eigo ga wakarimasu ka.**
  Does Mr. Takano understand English?

 B: **Ee, wakarimasu yo.**
  Yes, he does (lit., he understands).

The above does not apply to *Soo desu nee* or *Soo desu ka.*

(5) A: **Kore wa oishii desu nee.**
  This is delicious, isn't it!

 B: **Soo desu nee.**
  It is, isn't it!

(6) A: **Takada-san wa yoku nomimasu nee.**
  Mr. Takada drinks a lot, doesn't he!

 B: **Soo desu nee.**
  He does, doesn't he!

(7) A: **Kore wa oishii desu yo.**
  This is delicious, you know.

 B: **Soo desu ka.**
  Oh, is it?

(8) A: **Takada-san wa yoku nomimasu yo.**
  Mr. Takada drinks a lot, you know.

 B: **Soo desu ka.**
  Does he?

Incidentally, Japanese *soo* has etymologically nothing to do with English "so" although they sound alike and have similar meanings. Japanese *soo* is traceable to its older version *sayoo,* which has survived in the farewell *Sayoonara* "Good-by," which literally meant "If it is so [then we must part]." (See also SOO DESU KA.)

SOO DESU KA そうですか **Is that so?**

Soo desu ka "Is that so?" is a standard response to some-one's statement.

(1) A: **Kinoo Fuji-san ni nobotte-kimashita.**

　　　Yesterday I went climbing Mt. Fuji.

　 B: **Soo desu ka.**

　　　Is that so?

Since *Soo desu ka* is just a response and not a real question (though it looks like a question, with *ka* at the end), pronounce it with a falling intonation. If it is pronounced with a rising intonation, it becomes a genuine question meaning "Is what you've just said really so?" You would then sound as though you were questioning the other person's credibility.

Also remember that, in Japanese, *Soo desu ka* is probably used much more often than "Is that so?" in English. The reason is that *Soo desu ka* does not have many variants while "Is that so?" does. Consider the following examples in English:

(2) A: He's a great athlete.

　 B: Is he?

(3) A: My wife left for Europe yesterday.

　 B: Did she?

(4) A: Mr. Smith can speak Japanese, you know.

　 B: Can he?

All the responses above would be *Soo desu ka* in Japanese.

Soo desu ka does have a few variants, however, one being *Hontoo desu ka* (lit., "Is that a truth?"). *Hontoo desu ka,* as explained by Jorden (1, p. 29), "indicates livelier interest and greater surprise." It should, like *Soo desu ka,* be pronounced with a falling intonation unless you wish to indicate doubt.

SUKI 好き **to like**

Although *suki* is a *na*-noun and not a verb, it often corresponds to the English verb "like." It is probably used more commonly in reference to things than persons.

(1) **Wakai hito wa sakana yori niku no hoo ga suki desu.**
   Young people like meat better than fish.

Although *suki* may be used concerning people, as in (2) below, other expressions such as *ii* "good, nice" are probably used more frequently, as in (3), to express the same idea.

(2) **Kimi no otoo-san ga suki da.**
   I like your father.

(3) **Kimi no otoo-san ii hito da ne.**
   lit., Your father is a nice man.

This is, I suspect, due to Japanese speakers' preference for describing a person objectively over mentioning their subjective feelings toward him. In fact, *suki* used with reference to a person often means more than just "like." It means "love."

(4) Man: **Kimi ga suki da.**
   I love you.
   Woman: **Watashi mo anata ga suki yo.**
   I love you too.

(For Japanese expressions of love, see AISURU.)

Suki, unlike English "like," cannot refer to momentary liking. In English, one can say, for example,

(5) I liked the movie I saw yesterday.

In Japanese, on the other hand, *suki* cannot be used in such a context.

(6) **Kinoo mita eiga ga suki datta.*
   lit., I liked the movie I saw yesterday.

Instead, one would have to say something like

(7) **Kinoo mita eiga wa yokatta** (or **omoshirokatta**).
   The movie I saw yesterday was good (*or* fun).

Suki refers to liking something over a longer period of time, for example:

(8) **Eiga ga suki desu.**
I like movies.

(9) **Kinoo mita yoo na eiga ga suki desu.**
I like movies such as the one I saw yesterday.

SUKOSHI 少し a little, a few

Unlike *sukunai* "little, few," *sukoshi* has no negative overtone.

(1) **Mada okane ga sukoshi aru.**
I still have a little money.

(2) **Kinoo wa ooki na hon'ya e itta no de, sukoshi hon o katta.**
Since I went to a large bookstore yesterday, I bought some books.

Since *sukoshi* itself does not carry a negative connotation, in order to convey the idea of "not many" with *sukoshi,* one has to place the word in negative constructions, such as *shika . . . nai.*

(3) **Kyoo wa gakusei ga sukoshi shika konakatta.**
Only a few students came today.

Sentence (3) is very similar in meaning to (4).

(4) **Kyoo kita gakusei wa sukunakatta.**
The number of students who came today was small.

Note that in order to express the same idea, *sukoshi* has to be placed in a negative sentence, whereas *sukunai,* which carries a negative overtone, does not (see SUKUNAI).

SUKUNAI 少ない little, few

Sukunai is the opposite of *ooi* "much, many" (see OOI) and carries the negative overtone of "not much, not many."

(1) **Nihon ni wa yuden ga sukunai.**
    Japan has few oil fields.
(2) **Mochigane mo sukunaku natta.**
    I don't have much money left with me.

As is the case with *ooi*, *sukunai* cannot directly modify a noun that follows. For example, *sukunai hon does not normally mean "few books." Therefore, to express "I have few books," one cannot say

(3) **Sukunai hon o motte-imasu.*

The above sentence should be changed, for example, to

(4) **Watashi ga motte-iru hon wa sukunai desu.**
    lit., The books I have are few.

The combination *sukunai hon* can occur, however, in environments such as (5), where the item that is scarce is not the *hon* "book," but something else.

(5) **Kore wa goshoku no sukunai hon desu.**
    This is a book with few misprints.

SUMU 住む to live [somewhere]

Sumu is usually translated as "live" (in the sense of "to reside"), but it does not function exactly like "live." For example, *Nihon ni sumimasu* (lit. "I live in Japan") does not mean "I live in Japan." To express "I live in Japan," one must use the gerund form.

(1) **Nihon ni sunde-imasu.**
    I live in Japan.

Nihon ni sumimasu would only mean "I am going to live in Japan."

English "live" means both "to reside" and "to be alive." *Sumu*, however, does not cover this second meaning. In Japanese, this meaning is expressed by another verb, *ikiru*.

(2) **Chichi wa moo nakunarimashita ga, haha wa mada ikite-imasu** (not *sunde-imasu*).

My father is already dead, but my mother is still living.

SURU する to do

In English, "do" is both a real verb, as in (1), and an auxiliary verb used in place of another verb, as in (2), where "do" replaces the verb "drink."

(1) I do my homework every day.

(2) My wife drinks coffee, and I do too.

Japanese *suru,* on the other hand, functions only as a real verb and cannot by itself function in replacement of another verb. *Suru* is therefore correct in sentence (3), but not in (4).

(3) **Mainichi shukudai o suru.**

I do my homework every day.

(4) **Kanai mo koohii o nomu shi, watashi mo nomu** (not *suru*).

My wife drinks coffee, and I drink coffee too.

Suru as a verb, however, has a great variety of uses, many of which do not correspond to the uses of English "do."

(5) **Aoi kao o shite-iru.** (appearances)

He looks pale. (lit., He is doing a pale face.)

(6) **Isha o shite-iru.** (occupations)

He is a doctor. (lit., He is doing a doctor.)

(7) **Yoku seki o suru.** (physiological phenomena)

He often coughs. (lit., He often does a cough.)

(8) **Nekutai o shite-iru.** (certain items to wear)

He is wearing a necktie. (lit., He is doing a necktie.)

(9) **Mainichi tenisu o suru.** (activities)

He plays tennis every day. (lit., He does tennis every day.)

In addition to functioning as a transitive verb, as in the above sentences, *suru* is also used as an intransitive verb, as in the following:

(10) **Hen na oto ga suru.**
I hear a strange sound.

(11) **Nan ni suru**? (at a restaurant, asking a family member)
What will you have?

Suru is an extremely convenient word in that it can create new verbs by being attached to nouns. This is particularly the case with the ever-increasing number of verbs based on loanwords, e.g., *hassuru-suru* "to hustle" (i.e., "to move about briskly") and *taipu-suru* "to type." (Morita, pp. 248–55.)

SUZUSHII 涼しい [pleasantly] cool

In English, "cool" does not always refer to a pleasant temperature. *Suzushii,* on the other hand, always does. *Suzushii* therefore may be construed as corresponding to "pleasantly cool" rather than "cool" by itself.

Another important difference between "cool" and *suzushii* is that *suzushii* may not modify nouns that represent solids and fluids, whereas "cool" may. Of the following examples, therefore, (1) and (2) are correct, but (3) and (4) are not.

(1) **suzushii kaze**
a [pleasantly] cool wind

(2) **suzushii tenki**
[pleasantly] cool weather

(3) **suzushii nomimono*
something cool to drink

(4) **teeburu no suzushii hyoomen*
the cool surface of the table

To make (3) and (4) correct, one would have to use *tsumetai* "cold" (see TSUMETAI) instead of *suzushii*.

Like other temperature-related adjectives such as *samui* "cold" (see SAMUI), *atatakai* "warm" (see ATATAKAI), and *atsui* "hot" (see ATSUI), *suzushii* is closely connected with the change of seasons in Japan. *Suzushii* is tied with *aki* "fall," just as *samui* "cold" and *fuyu* "winter," *atatakai* "warm" and *haru* "spring," and *atsui* "hot" and *natsu* "summer" are inseparable pairs. *Suzushii* is most appropriately used when there is a pleasant drop in temperature following a hot day or a hot season. One says *Suzushii desu nee* "Isn't it nice and cool!" when, for example, there is a cool breeze at the end of a hot summer day, or when there is a nice cool day after the long hot summer months. In this sense, *suzushii* is different from "cool," which represents a temperature range between "cold" and "warm" and may be used regardless of preceding temperatures.

TABAKO たばこ, タバコ **cigarette**

Since *tabako* came into Japanese from Portuguese so long ago (i.e., in the 16th century), the fact that it was originally a foreign word is no longer felt very strongly. That is the reason *tabako* is often written in *hiragana* instead of in *katakana,* which are used for more recent loanwords.

Tabako originally meant "tobacco," but nowadays it usually refers to cigarettes, since they are the most common form of smoking material now.

The verb for "to smoke [a cigarette, tobacco, a cigar, etc.]" is *nomu* (lit., "to swallow") or *suu* (lit., "to inhale").

(1) **Anmari tabako o nomu (or suu) no wa karada ni yokunai.**
   "Smoking too much is not good for the health."

TABERU 食べる **to eat**

Taberu means "to eat," but there are at least two usage differences between *taberu* and "eat." First, as a rule, one "eats" soup in English, but "drinks" it in Japanese.

(1) **Nihon no inaka de wa maiasa misoshiru o nomu** (not *taberu).

In rural areas in Japan, they have (lit., drink) *miso* soup every morning.

Second, in English, one may either "have" or "eat" a meal. In Japanese, one "does" a meal.

(2) **Nihonjin wa futsuu mainichi san-do shokuji o suru** (not *taberu).

Japanese usually have (lit., do) three meals a day.

(However, if *gohan* is used instead of *shokuji* to mean "meal," *taberu* is the correct verb, as in *Moo gohan o tabemashita* "I've already eaten a meal.")

-TACHI たち (pluralizing suffix)

-Tachi is a pluralizing suffix.

(1) **gakusei-tachi**
    students

It may not be attached to nouns representing inanimate objects, nor is it added to nouns referring to animate beings other than humans. Therefore, (2) and (3) below are incorrect.

(2) *hon-tachi
    books

(3) *inu-tachi
    dogs

The use of *-tachi* is often not obligatory. It is dropped

when its absence does not make the meaning of the sentence unclear.

(4) **Kodomo** (not *Kodomo-tachi*) **ga futari imasu.**
I have two children.

-*Tachi* is different from the pluralizing suffix, "-s," in English in that it often means "and [the] others."

(5) **Tanaka-san-tachi ga kita.**
Mr. Tanaka and the others (*not* the Tanakas) have arrived.

(6) **Hayaku chichi-tachi ni kore o mise-tai.**
I'd like to show this to my father and the others (i.e., my mother and/or the other members of my family) at once.

TADAIMA ただいま **I'm home!**

Tadaima is a greeting used by a person who has just come home. In other words, it is an announcement of one's arrival at home. *Tadaima* is an abbreviation of *Tadaima kaerimashita* (lit., "I have returned just now"). Although this original sentence is still sometimes used on formal occasions, among family members it is almost always shortened to *Tadaima,* and most speakers are not even conscious of the original meaning of the word (i.e., "just now"), especially because the accent has changed. In the original sentence, the word is accented on the second syllable, whereas when used alone to mean "I'm home!" the accent shifts to the last syllable.

Tadaima is used every time one arrives home from school, work, shopping, or other outings, and the other members of the family respond to it by saying *Okaeri-nasai* meaning "Welcome home!" (see OKAERI-NASAI).

TAIHEN 大変 very, terrible, tremendous

Taihen, like *totemo* (see TOTEMO), means "very."

(1) **Kono natsu wa taihen** (or **totemo**) **atsukatta.**
    This summer was very hot.

Taihen used in this sense sounds more formal than *totemo,* which is relatively colloquial.

Taihen is sometimes used by itself or with *da* to mean "Something terrible has happened!" It is like an interjection.

(2) **Taihen da! Kaban o wasureta!**
    Good heavens! I forgot my briefcase!

When *taihen* modifies a noun, *na* comes in between. As a noun modifier, *taihen na* (somewhat like English "tremendous") may have either a good or a bad connotation, depending on the context.

(3) **taihen na gochisoo**
    a tremendous feast

(4) **taihen na atsusa**
    tremendous heat

TAKAI 高い expensive, high, tall

Takai meaning "expensive" is the opposite of *yasui* "inexpensive."

(1) **Anmari takai kara, kaemasen.**
    I can't buy it because it's too expensive.

Regarding height, *takai* means "high" or "tall." When used in this sense, *takai* is the opposite of *hikui* "low, short."

(2) **takai tana**
    high shelf

(3) **Hikooki ga takai tokoro o tonde-iru.**
    There's an airplane flying high up in the sky.

(4) **takai yama**
     high mountain
(5) **Asoko ni mieru ki wa zuibun takai desu nee.**
     The tree we can see over there is very tall, isn't it!
   To describe someone as being tall, we usually use *se ga takai* (lit., "the height is tall") instead of *takai* by itself.
(6) **Jonson-san wa se ga takai.**
     Mr. Johnson is tall (lit., Mr. Johnson's height is tall).
   To the surprise of English speakers, *takai* is also used in reference to some parts of the face when they protrude more than normal.
(7) **takai hana**
     long nose (lit., high nose)
(8) **takai hoobone**
     protruding cheekbones (lit., high cheek bones)

TAKUSAN たくさん **a lot, enough**

Takusan means "a lot" in the sense of "a great number" or "a great amount."
(1) **Asoko ni hito ga takusan iru.**
     There are a lot of people over there.
(2) **Hon o takusan kaita.**
     I wrote a lot of books.
   When *takusan* precedes a noun, *no* is required in between.
(3) **Takusan no hon o kaita.**
     I wrote a lot of books.
The pattern used in (3), however, is not as common as that used in (1) and (2), where *takusan* follows a noun with a particle in between.
   Takusan also means "enough." When used in this sense, it is often preceded by *moo* "already."

(4) **Sore dake areba, takusan desu.**
If I have that much, it should be enough.

(5) **Konna hanashi wa moo takusan da.**
I don't want to hear that kind of thing any more. (lit., I've already had enough of this kind of talk.)

Takusan meaning "enough" does not normally precede a noun. (See also OOI.)

TANI 谷 valley

Although *tani* is usually equated with English "valley," there is definitely a difference between the two. A valley can be either quite narrow or fairly wide, often corresponding to what one might call a *bonchi* "basin" in Japanese. A *tani,* on the other hand, is always a very narrow space between mountains with no or little flat area to speak of.

TANOSHII 楽しい happy, enjoyable

An experience one enjoys makes one feel *tanoshii*.

(1) **Gakusei-seikatsu wa tanoshii.**
Student life makes me happy. (*or* I'm enjoying student life.)

(2) **Tomodachi to hito-ban-juu nondari hanashitari-shite tanoshi katta.**
I was happy to spend the whole night drinking and talking with my friend. (*or* I enjoyed drinking and talking with my friend all night.)

Tanoshii refers to a sustained state of happiness. To express a momentary state of joy, use *ureshii* "glad, joyous."

(3) A: **Shiken ni pasu-shita toki wa donna kimochi deshita ka.**

How did you feel when you passed the exam?

B: **Ureshikatta** (not *tanoshikatta*) **desu.**

I was happy.

Tanoshii represents a sense of happiness due to one's own experience. Simply receiving the news of a happy event, for example, does not make one *tanoshii*.

(4) **Betonamu-sensoo ga owatta nyuusu o kiite ureshikatta** (not *tanoshikatta*).

I was happy to hear the news that the Vietnam War was over.

Tanoshii, as a rule, refers to the speaker's happy feeling, and no one else's. That is why sentence (5) is right while (6) is wrong.

(5) **Watashi wa mainichi tanoshii.**

I am happy every day.

(6) *Kojima-san wa mainichi tanoshii.*

Mr. Kojima is happy every day.

In Japanese, one just cannot make a definite statement like (5) about someone else's feeling unless one is a novelist manipulating a character in a novel. To convey the idea of "Mr. Kojima is happy every day" in Japanese, one would have to say one of the following:

(7) **Kojima-san wa mainichi** | (a) **tanoshi-soo da.**
| (b) **tanoshii rashii.**
| (b) **tanoshii yoo da.**

Mr. Kojima looks (*or* seems) happy every day.

This is true of other adjectives of emotion such as *kanashii* "sad," *sabishii* "lonely," and *ureshii*.

TASUKERU 助ける **to help**

Tasukeru is sometimes used in the sense of *tetsudau* "to help [someone] do [something, such as chores]." For example, in sentence (1), either *tasukeru* or *tetsudau* may be used without much difference in meaning.

(1) **Chichi no shigoto o tasukete-imasu** (or **tetsudatte-imasu**).
     I am helping my father with his work.

Tasukeru meaning "to help [someone] do [something]," however, is usually reserved for more than mere chores. A mother who is doing the dishes, for example, is likely to say to her daughter

(2) **Tetsudatte.** (rather than **Tasukete.*)
     Help me [with the dishes].

   Tasukeru also means "to help" in the sense of "to save, to relieve, to rescue [someone]" or "to spare [someone's life]." *Tetsudau* does not have such meanings, as in the following:

(3) **Shinu tokoro o ano hito ni tasukerareta.**
     I was saved (*or* rescued) by him from certain death.

(4) **Inochi dake wa tasukete-kudasai.**
     Please spare my life.

(5) **Byooki ni kurushimu hitobito o tasukeru no ga isha no tsutome da.**
     It is the doctor's obligation to relieve those suffering from illness.

Likewise, if you are about to be drowned or if you are attacked by a mugger, yell out

(6) **Tasukete!**
     Help!

If you yelled out *Tetsudatte!* no one would come to your rescue!

TATEMONO 建物 building

Tatemono literally means "built thing," and is a generic

term for buildings in general whether they are Japanese style or Western style. *Birudingu* (from English "building"), or more often *biru* for short, on the other hand, refers only to large Western-style buildings.

TENKI 天気 weather

Tenki and its polite form, *otenki,* mean "weather."
(1) **Kyoo wa ii otenki da.**
 We are having nice weather today.
(2) **Iya na otenki desu nee.**
 Nasty weather, isn't it!
 Interestingly enough, when used without specific modifiers such as *ii* "good" or *iya na* "nasty," *tenki* sometimes means "good weather."
(3) **Ashita wa otenki ni naru deshoo.**
 I think it's going to clear up tomorrow. (lit., It will probably become good weather tomorrow.)
This contrasts with English "weather," which, when used without "good" or "bad" modifying it, might mean "bad weather," as in "We have some weather coming our way."

TO 戸 door

To has a wider range of meaning than *doa* (from English "door"), which refers to Western-style doors only. Sliding doors such as those found at the entrance of a Japanese inn are therefore *to,* and not *doa.*

 When one talks about doors of all kinds, both Japanese and Western, *to* is the term to be used.
(1) **Yoru neru mae ni uchi-juu no to o yoku shimete-kudasai.**

Before you go to bed, be sure to lock all doors in the house.

When one refers specifically to a Western-style door, *doa* is more likely to be used than *to*.

(2) **Doa** (probably not *To) **no nobu ga torete-shimatta.** The doorknob has fallen off.

Doors of a Western-style vehicle (e.g., *densha* "electric train," *kuruma* "car," *erebeetaa* "elevator") are also *doa* rather than *to*.

TOKEI 時計 watch, clock

Any kind of timepiece is a *tokei*. Both clocks and watches are usually called *tokei* unless it becomes necessary to make a distinction between them. When it is necessary, however, we say *ude-dokei* "wristwatch," *kaichuu-dokei* "pocket watch," *oki-dokei* (the kind of clock you might find on a mantlepiece), *mezamashi-dokei* "alarm clock," etc.

TOKI 時 time

It seems that *toki* tends to refer to a shorter time span than English "time." This is particularly true of the expression *sono toki* (lit., "at that time") as compared with English "at that time." Suppose you have been talking about the early years of Meiji and now want to refer to the scarcity of Japanese who were familiar with English during that period. In English, you can use either (1a) or (1b) to express that idea.

(1) (a) In those days,
(b) At (*or* About) that time,
  not too many Japanese spoke English.

In Japanese, on the other hand, *sono toki* "at that time" would not be as appropriate as *sono koro* "about that time, in those days." (See also KORO.)

(2) |(a) **Sono koro**|
    |(b) *?Sono toki*|
    eigo no dekiru Nihonjin wa sukunakatta.

Sono toki is not quite appropriate since the time referred to is a span of several years which is not clearly defined. If, however, the time referred to were more specific, e.g., the time of the departure of the Iwakura Mission for the United States in 1872, *sono toki* would be perfectly correct. (See also JIKAN.)

TOMODACHI 友達 **friend**

The word *tomodachi* probably carries more weight in Japanese than "friend" does in English. In other words, becoming a *tomodachi* is much more difficult than becoming a friend. In fact, you almost have to go to school with someone and remain pretty close to him for some time before becoming his *tomodachi*. Even if you go to the same school with someone, you are his *senpai* "senior" (see SENPAI) if you are even one class ahead, and his *koohai* "junior" (see KOOHAI) if you are even one class behind. In neither case can you call yourself his *tomodachi*.

When someone graduates from college and starts working, he is surrounded at work by *senpai, koohai,* and *dooryoo* "colleagues at about the same seniority level." But he does not normally call them *tomodachi*. Among them, he might find some *nomi-tomodachi* "drinking pals," but they are still referred to by that compound rather than simply as *tomodachi*.

Some Americans in Japan ask Japanese how to say

"friend" in their language. Upon receiving the answer *tomodachi,* they start calling their Japanese acquaintances *tomodachi* or *watashi no tomodachi.* Those few Japanese who know English well enough realize that what these Americans are doing is simply translating "my friend" into Japanese, but others just feel uncomfortable, not knowing how to respond.

Some Americans also make the error of using *ii tomodachi* (lit., "good friend") as a direct translation of English "good friend" meaning "close friend." In Japanese, however, *ii tomodachi* does not mean "close friend," but rather "friend who is good, i.e., one who is reliable, faithful, helpful, and exerts good influence on you." "Good friend" in the sense of "close friend" is *shin'yuu.* As in the case of *tomodachi,* the Japanese speaker uses this word very sparingly. It is more like "closest friend."

TONARI 隣 next door, adjacent, adjoining

Tonari is used especially when two objects of more or less the same category are in question. When two objects belong to two entirely different categories, *tonari* is not appropriate. Examples (1) and (2) are therefore correct, but (3) and (4) sound very strange.

(1) **Sakanaya wa nikuya no tonari desu.**
    The fish market is next to the meat market.

(2) **Uchi no tonari ni Amerikajin no kazoku ga sunde-iru.**
    An American family is living next door to us (i.e., in the house next to ours).

(3) *?Boku no uchi wa ooki na sakura no ki no tonari desu.*
    My house is next to a huge cherry tree.

(4) *?Kadan no tonari ni inu ga nete-iru.*

There is a dog lying next to the flower bed.

In such cases as (3) and (4), *tonari* should be replaced by [*sugu*] *yoko* "by, at the side of."

In English, a person living next to you is a neighbor, but a person living several doors away is also a neighbor. In Japanese, however, only the former would be a *tonari no hito* (lit., "person next door"), whereas the latter would be a *kinjo no hito* (lit., "person in the neighborhood").

TOOI 遠い **far, distant**

Tooi can mean "far, distant" in terms of space, time, or relationships.

(1) **Boku no uchi wa eki kara tooi.** (space)
My house is far from the station.

(2) **Sore wa tooi shoorai no koto da.** (time)
That is a matter of the distant future.

(3) **Kare wa boku no tooi shinseki da.** (relationship)
He is a distant relative of mine.

In example (1) above, *kara* "from" may be replaced by *made* "as far as," as in (4), with only a slight difference in meaning.

(4) **Boku no uchi wa eki made tooi.**
It is a long distance from my house to the station.

There are some interesting uses of *tooi*.

(5) **Ano hito wa mimi ga tooi.**
He is hard of hearing. (lit., As for him, the ears are far, i.e., All sounds are like faraway sounds to him.)

(6) **Denwa ga tooi desu kara, ooki na koe de hanashite-kudasai.**
Since your voice on the phone is faint (lit., faraway), please talk louder.

⌐
TOOTOO とうとう finally, at last, in the end, after all

Tootoo is used when something eventually materializes (or fails to materialize) after a long process. It is neutral with regard to the desirability or undesirability of the final outcome.

(1) **Ano genki na Mori-san mo tootoo byooki ni natta.**
   That tough Mr. Mori, too, has finally taken ill.

(2) **Takahashi-san wa nagai aida dokushin datta ga, tootoo kekkon-shita.**
   Mr. Takahashi was a bachelor for a long time, but he finally got married.

(2) **Zuibun matte-ita no ni tootoo kimasendeshita.**
   I waited for a long time, but he never showed up (lit., he didn't come after all).

(See also YATTO.)

TOTEMO とても very

Totemo has two basic uses. First, it means "very," as in (1) and (2), where it modifies an adjective and a *na*-noun, respectively.

(1) **Kyoo wa totemo samui.**
   It's very cold today.

(2) **Yamada-san wa totemo shinsetsu na hito da.**
   Mr. Yamada is a very kind person.

Totemo may also modify some verbs.

(3) **Totemo komatta.**
   I was quite at a loss.

According to Morita (p. 324), only verbs that describe states may be modified by *totemo*. That is why we cannot use, for example, **Totemo hataraita* to mean "I worked very hard." (To express the idea of "I worked very hard," an entirely different word would have to be used: *Isshooken-mei hataraita.)*

Unlike "very," *totemo* meaning "very" cannot be used with a negative word. Compare the following examples:

(4) It is not very cold today.

(5) **Kyoo wa totemo samukunai.*

lit., It is not very cold today.

While (4) is perfectly grammatical, (5) is ungrammatical. Sentence (5) becomes grammatical if *totemo* is replaced by *amari* "too" (see AMARI).

(6) **Kyoo wa amari samukunai.**

It is not too cold today.

The second use of *totemo* is to modify a negative verb or a *na*-noun with a negative meaning to signify "[cannot] possibly" or "[not] by any means."

(7) **Konna muzukashii mondai wa watashi ni wa totemo wakarimasen.**

I cannot possibly understand such a difficult problem.

(8) **Sore wa boku ni wa totemo muri da.**

I cannot possibly do that.

There are several synonyms for *totemo* meaning "very," e.g., *hijoo ni* and *taihen*. In (1) through (3) above, these two words can be used in place of *totemo,* as in

(9) **Kyoo wa hijoo ni** (or **taihen**) **samui.**

It is very cold today.

Of these three words, *totemo* is the most colloquial, *taihen* is more formal, and *hijoo ni* the most formal (see TAIHEN).

Totemo has a variant, *tottemo,* which is even more colloquial than *totemo* and perhaps more emphatic as well.

TSUGOO GA II 都合がいい convenient

Tsugoo ga ii "convenient" literally means "circumstances

are good" and should be clearly distinguished from *benri*
"convenient." *Benri* means "handy, accessible, convenient
to use," while *tsugoo ga ii* indicates that "stated conditions
are convenient for someone on a particular occasion" (Jorden, 2, p. 185). In sentence (1) only *benri* is correct, whereas
in (2) only *tsugoo ga ii* can be used.

(1) **Denkigama wa benri** (not *tsugoo ga ii) **desu nee.**
    Aren't electric rice cookers handy?
(2) **Pikunikku ga ashita da to tsugoo ga ii** (not *benri) **n desu
    ga.**
    It would be convenient for me if the picnic were sched-
    uled for tomorrow.

TSUMA 妻 wife

Tsuma is normally a written form.

(1) **bushi no tsuma**
    the wives of samurai

In conversation, one would use *samurai no okusan* to mean
"the wives of samurai."

In spoken Japanese, *tsuma* is sometimes used to refer to
one's own wife, but it sounds very formal and somewhat
stilted. It is not used as commonly as other variants meaning "my wife," such as *kanai* (see KANAI).

TSUMARANAI つまらない uninteresting, insignificant

Tsumaranai most often means "dull, uninteresting, no fun."

(1) **Ano eiga wa tsumaranai kara, minai hoo ga ii.**
    That movie is dull; you'd better not see it.
(2) **Kinoo no paatii wa tsumaranakatta.**

Yesterday's party was no fun.

When used in this sense, *tsumaranai* is the opposite of *omoshiroi* "interesting, fun."

Tsumaranai also means "insignificant" or "trivial."

(3) **Tsumaranai koto de okotte wa ikenai.**

One should not get angry over trivial matters.

Tsumaranai meaning "insignificant" often appears as part of the set phrase *Konna tsumaranai mono de shitsurei desu ga* (lit., "Forgive me for such an insignificant gift"), a cliché but nonetheless a still enormously popular expression used by gift givers as they present gifts. English speakers, when first coming across this expression, might feel it is hypocritical of Japanese to call all gifts *tsumaranai,* for some could be quite special or expensive. The reason the Japanese speaker uses this phrase, however, is not because he is hypocritical but because he does not want the receiver to feel obligated.

Although these two meanings of *tsumaranai* may sound totally unrelated, they are actually not that far apart. Dull things are often trivial and insignificant, and trivial and insignificant things of course fail to interest anyone.

TSUMETAI 冷たい **cold**

Unlike *samui,* which refers to a sensation of coldness affecting the whole body (see SAMUI), *tsumetai* represents a sensation of coldness perceived by the skin only or by a limited portion of one's body. *Tsumetai* is therefore especially appropriate when used in reference to solids and fluids, as in

(1) **tsumetai juusu**
cold juice

(2) **tsumetai te**
cold hand

When one takes a cold shower, the first sensation perceived by the skin makes one shout *Tsumetai!* If, however, one feels chilled after the cold shower, one might say, shivering, *Samui!*

TSUTOMERU 勤める **to become employed**

Tsutomeru is often given as "to work" in textbooks and dictionaries, but Jorden (1, p. 149) is a happy exception. She explains *tsutomeru* as "become employed" and *tsutomete-iru* as "be employed." If all textbooks and dictionaries followed her example, fewer students of Japanese would be using

(1) **Yoshida-san wa ginkoo ni tsutomemasu.**

to mean "Mr. Yoshida works for a bank." Sentence (1), however, can only mean "Mr. Yoshida will be working for (lit., will be employed at) a bank." To mean "Mr. Yoshida works for a bank," one should use

(2) **Yoshida-san wa ginkoo ni tsutomete-imasu.**

lit., Mr. Yoshida has become employed at a bank.

Ginkoo ni tsutomete-iru "to work for a bank" should also be clearly distinguished from *ginkoo de hataraite-iru* "to be working at a bank." (See also HATARAKU.)

UCHI うち **home, house**

Uchi is quite similar in meaning to *ie* (see IE). For example, in sentence (1) below, *uchi* and *ie* are more or less interchangeable.

(1) **Ano hito wa zuibun ookii uchi** (or **ie**) **o katta.**

He bought a very large house.

The only difference in this case—at least, to a Tokyoite—

is that *uchi* is more colloquial while *ie* is more formal.

There are some situations where *uchi* is preferred to *ie* (Matsuo et al., pp. 35–36). For example, when one refers to one's own home, *uchi* is more appropriate.

(2) **Yuube wa uchi ni imashita.**
I was at home yesterday.

(3) **Uchi e kaette mo ii desu ka.**
May I go home?

Uchi no (but not *ie no) is often used to mean "my" or "our" when referring to one's own family members or family belongings.

(4) **uchi no musuko (musume, inu, kuruma,** etc.)
my (*or* our) son (daughter, dog, car, etc.)

Uchi is sometimes used as an abbreviation of *uchi no shujin* "my husband." *Ie* has no such usage.

(5) **Uchi** (not *Ie) **wa itsumo kaeri ga osoi n desu.**
My husband always comes home late.

UMAI う ま い skillful, delicious

Umai has two basic meanings: skillful," as in (1), and "delicious," as in (2).

(1) **Ano hito wa gorufu ga umai.**
He is good at golf.

(2) **Kono sakana wa umai.**
This fish is delicious.

In the sense of "skillful," *umai* is synonymous with *joozu,* but, according to Tokugawa and Miyajima (p. 54), *umai* is a little more colloquial than *joozu.*

In the sense of "delicious," *umai* is synonymous with *oishii,* but *umai* is used only by men, and in rather informal situations.

UNTENSHU 運転手 driver

An *untenshu* is a person who operates or drives a vehicle for a living. The English counterpart could be "driver," "motorman," or "engineer," depending on the type of vehicle. *Untenshu* might also mean "chauffeur."

Unless a person operates or drives a vehicle for a living, he cannot be called *untenshu*. In English, anyone who drives well may be referred to as a good driver. In Japanese, on the other hand, *joozu na untenshu* means "skillful professional driver." If someone who is not a driver by occupation happens to drive well, we say

(1) **Ano hito wa unten ga joozu da.**
    He is good at driving.

URUSAI うるさい noisy, fussy, bothersome

Urusai most frequently means "noisy."

(1) **Tonari no rajio wa urusai desu nee!**
    Isn't the radio next door noisy!

Urusai might also mean "fussy," since a fussy person makes noise by fussing about trivial things.

(2) **Yamamoto-sensei wa komakai koto ni urusai.**
    Professor Yamamoto is fussy about little details.

Urusai in the sense of "noisy" is often used as a warning to someone who is too noisy. It is extremely interesting that in English an adjective with the opposite meaning, "quiet," would be used in a similar situation.

(3) **Urusai!** (i.e., You're noisy, [so be quiet]!)
    Quiet! (i.e., [You're noisy, so be] quiet!)

Urusai sometimes means "bothersome, annoying" also.

(4) **Kinjo-zukiai ga urusai.**

Getting along with the neighbors is bothersome.

There is a synonym for *urusai, yakamashii.* In the sense of "noisy" or "fussy," these two adjectives may be used more or less interchangeably, but *yakamashii* can never mean "bothersome." In other words, although *urusai* can be replaced by *yakamashii* in (1), (2), and (3) above, it cannot in (4).

USHI 牛 cattle, bull, cow, ox, steer

Since the English have long been a cattle-raising people, their language is replete with terms referring to different types of bovines such as "cattle," "bull," "cow," "ox," and "steer." The Japanese, on the other hand, have never been a cattle-raising people, and their language reflects this fact by having only one word, *ushi,* to refer to all bovines. When the Japanese speaker must be specific about different types of *ushi,* he simply adds different prefixes to make compounds, such as *o-ushi* "male *ushi,*" *me-ushi* "female *ushi,*" and *kyo-sei-ushi* "castrated *ushi.*"

"Beef," however, is not called *ushi,* but *gyuu-niku* (*gyuu* being another reading of the *kanji* for *ushi,* plus *niku* "meat") or simply *gyuu.* A loanword, *biifu* (from English "beef"), is also used in the sense of "beef," but usually in compounds such as *roosuto-biifu* "roast beef" and *biifu-shichuu* "beef stew."

UTSUKUSHII 美しい beautiful

Although *utsukushii* is regularly equated with English "beautiful," it is far less conversational than the latter. For example, *utsukushii onna-no-hito* "beautiful women" and *utsukushii keshiki* "beautiful view" are perfectly all right in writing, but a little unnatural in conversation. Most speakers of Japanese would rather say *kirei na onna-no-hito* and *kirei na keshiki* instead.

Utsukushii basically describes something that is pleasing to the eye or the ear (e.g., *utsukushii hana* "beautiful flower" and *utsukushii ongaku* "beautiful music"), and, on limited occasions, to the heart (e.g., *utsukushii hanashi* "beautifully moving story"). It does not have as wide a range of meaning as "beautiful," which is frequently used, especially in colloquial English, to mean "excellent, terrific, super" (e.g., "a beautiful opportunity," "a beautiful plan").

Unlike *kirei, utsukushii* cannot mean "clean." *Kirei,* on the other hand, cannot mean "beautifully moving," as *utsukushii* does.

WAKAI 若い young

Unlike "young," *wakai* cannot be used to describe children. In English, little children may be called young, but *wakai* is used for people who are at least in their upper teens. In other words, until one becomes old enough to become a *wakai hito* "young adult," one is simply a *kodomo* "child," not a *wakai kodomo*.

Although *wakai* as a rule modifies only animate beings such as *hito* "person," it is sometimes used with reference to serial numbers to mean "smaller." For example, No. 23 is a *wakai bangoo* "smaller number" (lit., "young number") in comparison with No. 24.

WAKARU 分かる to understand

Wakaru means "[something] is clear" or "to become clear

[to someone]." That is why the particle preceding *wakaru* is *ga* instead of *o*. When *wakaru* is translated into English, however, the most natural equivalent is often either "understand" or "know."

(1) **Nishio-san wa Roshiago ga wakaru.**

   Mr. Nishio understands Russian.

(2) **Ano hito ga naze konakatta ka wakaranai.**

   I don't understand (*or* know) why he didn't come. (lit., Why he didn't come is not clear to me.)

(3) A: **Ima nan-ji deshoo ka.**

   What time is it?

   B: **Chotto wakarimasen ga.**

   Sorry but I don't know. (lit., It's a bit unclear to me.)

Since *wakaru* means "[something] is *or* becomes clear," it represents an event that is not controllable by the speaker. *Wakaru* consequently cannot take a potential form, i.e., there is no such form as **wakareru* to mean "[something] can be *or* become clear."

In example (3) above, *Wakarimasen,* meaning "I don't know," may be replaced by *Shirimasen,* which also means "I don't know." But there is a difference between the two. According to Mizutani and Mizutani (1, p. 57), *Shirimasen* means "I haven't had the chance to get the information," while *Wakarimasen* is used when the speaker feels he should know the answer. Therefore, as a rule, avoid *Shirimasen* as an answer to a question about yourself. For example,

(4) A: **Kondo no shuumatsu ni wa nani o suru tsumori desu ka.**

   What do you plan to do this weekend?

   B: **Wakarimasen.** (not **Shirimasen.*)

   I don't know.

Wakarimasen in this case implies "I should know the answer but I'm sorry I don't," and is therefore a proper answer, whereas *Shirimasen* might even indicate "This sort of thing has nothing to do with me," and is therefore inappropriate.

The past-tense form *Wakarimashita* often means "I have understood what you just said" (Jorden, 1, p. 78). This usage occurs especially as a response to an explanation or request.

(5) Professor: **Kono teepu-rekoodaa rabo ni kaeshite-oite-kuremasen ka. Kyoo wa rabo ga yasumi dakara, ashita no asa ne.**

Would you mind returning this tape recorder to the lab? The lab is closed today, so do it tomorrow morning, will you?

Student: **Wakarimashita.**

I'll be glad to. (lit., I understood you[r request and will gladly accommodate it].)

(See also SHIRU and RIKAI-SURU.)

WAREWARE 我々 we

Wareware is more formal than *watakushi-tachi* or *watashi-tachi,* both of which mean the same thing. It is more suited to writing or formal speech.

(1) **Wareware wa kuni no tame ni tachi-agaranakereba naranai.**

We must rise for the sake of our country.

WARUI 悪い bad

Warui is used not only to refer to things or persons that are "bad," like *warui tenki* "bad weather" and *warui ko* "a bad child," but is sometimes used to express gratitude, as in sentence (1) below. (When used in this sense, *warui* does not normally precede a noun.)

(1) **Kekkoo na mono o itadaite warui desu nee.**

Thank you for giving me such a nice present.

The reason *warui* is used as an expression of gratitude is probably that Japanese people often feel guilty about a favor done for them. For them, receiving a favor from someone is like having inconvenienced that person, who must have spent time and/or money on it. This guilty feeling is what is behind the expression *Warui desu nee.*

WATASHI わたし I

Watashi (and its even more formal variant, *watakushi*) is a "personal pronoun" used by a speaker to refer to himself. Males hardly ever use it when they are young because they use *boku* instead (see BOKU). They begin using *watashi* immediately after they graduate from college and start working. They use it on formal occasions, especially in talking to people higher in status. Females start using *watashi* (or more colloquially, *atashi*) as children and use it throughout their lives. The frequency of *watashi* in Japanese, however, is minuscule compared with that of "I," "my," and "me" in English, since Japanese speakers, instead of using "pronouns," would rather use the context to make it clear that they are talking about themselves, as in the following example:

(1) **Ashita [watashi no] uchi e irasshaimasen ka.**

Would you like to come to my house tomorrow?

In this case, while "my" would be obligatory in English, *watashi no* meaning "my" is optional and most likely to be left out in Japanese.

YARU やる **to do**

Yaru, when used in the sense of "to do," is synonymous with *suru*.

(1) **Ban-gohan no ato de sugu shukudai o** | (a) **yaru.**
                                              | (b) **suru.**

   I do my homework right after dinner.

Both (a) and (b) mean the same thing. The only difference is that *yaru* is a little more conversational than *suru* (Tokugawa and Miyajima, p. 217).

   Yaru cannot be attached to nouns to form compound verbs, whereas *suru* can.

(2) **benkyoo-suru** (not *benkyoo-yaru. However, *benkyoo o yaru* would be acceptable.)
   to study

   Yaru and *suru* are not always interchangeable. *Yaru,* for example, also means "to give [to a lower-status person]," as in *Musuko ni pen o yatta* "I gave my son a pen," but *suru* does not have that meaning. Of the sample sentences given under *suru* (see SURU), (6) and (9) can definitely take *yaru* instead of *suru,* and (7) and (8) can probably take *yaru,* but (5) is definitely unacceptable. Since *yaru* has no intransitive uses, it cannot replace *suru* in (10) and (11).

YASASHII やさしい **gentle, easy**

Yasashii has two meanings: "gentle," as in (1), and "easy," as in (2).

(1) **Ano hito wa yasashii.**
   That person is gentle.

(2) **Ano mondai wa yasashii.**
   That question is easy.

"Easy" and "gentle" may seem far apart in meaning to English speakers, but they really are not that distant if one stretches one's imagination a little. After all, it is easy to deal with gentle people, and easy problems keep you gentle!

When *yasashii* means "easy," it is normally not used adverbially. Sentence (3) below is therefore incorrect.

(3) **Kodomo de mo yasashiku dekiru.*

    Even children can do it easily.

Yasashiku in (3) should be replaced by *kantan ni* "simply, easily."

(4) **Kodomo de mo kantan ni dekiru.**

    Even children can do it easily.

YASUI 安い inexpensive

Yasui "inexpensive" is the opposite of *takai* meaning "expensive."

(1) **Ano mise ni wa takai mono wa aru ga yasui mono wa nai.**

    That store has expensive things but not inexpensive things.

(When *takai* means "high" or "tall," however, the opposite is not *yasui* but *hikui*.) (See HIKUI.)

Yasui means "easy," too, but mainly in the set phrase *Oyasui goyoo desu* "I'll be happy to do that for you" (lit., "That's an easy thing to do"), an expression of willingness to meet someone's request. Ordinarily, *yasashii* is the word for "easy" (see YASASHII).

Yasui in the sense of "easy" is also used in combination with the stem of a verb, as in *yomi-yasui* "easy to read," *oboe-yasui* "easy to learn," etc.

YASUMI 休み **vacation, absence**

Yasumi comes from the verb *yasumu* meaning "to rest" or "not to work." It therefore corresponds to a wide range of English words such as "absence," "recess," "vacation," "day off," and "holiday."

(1) **Hiru-yasumi ni resutoran e itta.**
I went to a restaurant during the noon recess.

(2) **Suzuki-san wa kyoo yasumi da ga doo shita n daroo.**
Mr. Suzuki is absent today. I wonder what's happened to him.

(3) **Kotoshi no natsu-yasumi ni wa doko e ikimasu ka.**
Where are you going during the summer vacation this year?

(4) **Ashita yasumi o toroo to omotte-iru.**
I'm thinking of taking the day off tomorrow.

(5) **Nihon de wa Kurisumasu no hi wa yasumi desu ka.**
Is Christmas Day a holiday in Japan?

YATTO やっと **finally**

Although *yatto* and *tootoo* (see TOOTOO) are both translated into English as "finally," they are not the same. First of all, *yatto* cannot be used when something fails to materialize. In (1), therefore, only *tootoo* is correct.

(1) **Tegami wa kyoo mo tootoo** (not *yatto) **konakatta.**
The letter didn't arrive today either despite all my waiting.

Second, while *tootoo* is neutral as to the desirability or undesirability of the final outcome, *yatto* is used only when the result is desirable. In sentence (2), therefore, only *tootoo* is correct.

(2) **Hitori, futari to shinde-itte, tootoo** (not *yatto) **minna shinde-shimatta.**

They died one by one until finally they were all dead. (In sentence 2 above, yatto would be correct if the speaker, for some reason or another, had wanted all of these people to die.)

When yatto and tootoo are used with regard to a desirable outcome, they are quite similar, but there is a slight difference in connotation.

(3) **Mai-tsuki chokin-shite-ita okane ga tootoo** (or **yatto**) **hyakuman-en ni natta.**

The money that I've been saving every month has finally reached the sum of 1,000,000 yen.

In this case, tootoo signals that the speaker is reporting objectively on the eventual outcome of a particular event; how he feels about the outcome is not the issue. Yatto, on the other hand, implies that the speaker has been looking forward to this outcome for some time.

YOBU 呼ぶ to call

First, yobu means "to call" in the sense of "to call out" or "to call by name."

(1) **"Morita-san!" to yonda no ni henji o shinakatta.**

I called out, "Mr. Morita!" but he didn't answer.

Second, yobu means "to call" in the sense of "to give someone (or something) the name of."

(2) **Nyuuyooku wa naze biggu-appuru to yobareru no daroo ka.**

I wonder why New York is called "the Big Apple."

Third, yobu means "to call" in the sense of "to send for" or "to summon."

(3) **Kanai ga byooki ni natta no de, isha o yonda.**

I sent for the doctor because my wife became ill.

In English, "call" can mean "to telephone" or "to make a short visit." *Yobu* does not have those meanings. In (4) below, only (b) is correct.

(4) (a) **Yobimashita ga,*

(b) **Denwa o kakemashita ga,** ohanashi-chuu deshita.

I called that number, but the line was busy.

Unlike "call," *yobu* is often used to mean "to invite."

(5) **Ashita Matsuda-san o yuushoku ni yoboo.**

Let's invite Mr. Matsuda [to our house] for dinner tomorrow.

YOKU よく often

Yoku, the adverbial form of *yoi* (or *ii*), is frequently used to mean "often."

(1) **Yoku eiga e ikimasu.**

I often go to the movies.

(2) **Konogoro wa yoku ame ga furu.**

It often rains these days.

However, *yoku* should not be used in the negative. The following sentence is wrong.

(3) **Yoshimoto-san wa yoku eiga e ikimasen.*

Mr. Yoshimoto does not go to the movies often.

To make (3) correct, *yoku* must be replaced by *amari* (see AMARI).

(4) **Yoshimoto-san wa amari eiga e ikimasen.**

Mr. Yoshimoto does not go to the movies often (lit., much).

Since *yoku* is the adverbial form of *yoi* (or *ii*) meaning "good," it may be used in the sense of "well."

(5) **Yuube wa yoku neta.**
I slept very well last night.

However, while "well" may be used in the sense of "skill-fully," as in "Mr. Smith speaks Japanese very well," *yoku* often cannot be used in this sense. Sentence (6) below, for example, is wrong if the speaker wants it to mean "Mr. Smith speaks Japanese very well."

(6) *Sumisu-san wa Nihongo o yoku hanasu.*

This sentence is correct only in the sense of "Mr. Smith often speaks Japanese." The Japanese equivalent of "Mr. Smith speaks Japanese very well" would be, for example,

(7) **Sumisu-san wa Nihongo o hanasu no ga joozu da.**
lit., Mr. Smith is good at speaking Japanese.

(8) **Sumisu-san wa Nihongo ga joozu ni hanaseru.**
lit., Mr. Smith can speak Japanese very well.

-YOOBI 曜日 day of the week

In Japanese, the names of the days of the week all have *-yoobi* (or *-yoo* for short) at the end, e.g., *nichi-yoobi, getsu-yoobi,* etc. There is a significant difference in usage between these Japanese terms and their English counterparts, for the Japanese speaker does not seem to use these names as often as the English speaker does the English terms. The reason is that Japanese speakers are often more comfortable re-ferring to a particular day by its date than by its day of the week. For example, while an American might say "I'm get-ting married two weeks from this Friday," using the name of a day of the week, a Japanese in a corresponding situation would be more likely to refer to the date of the same day and say, for example, *Kongetsu no juuhachi-nichi ni kek-kon-shimasu* "I'm getting married on the 18th of this month."

⌐YOROKOBU⌐ 喜ぶ **to rejoice, to be glad**

Yorokobu, like *ureshii,* can often be equated with English "be glad," as in

(a) **Kitagawa-san wa sono shirase o kiite yorokonda.**

Mr. Kitagawa was glad to hear the news.

There is, however, a crucial difference between *yorokobu* and *ureshii* beyond the fact that the former is a verb and the latter an adjective. *Ureshii,* like other adjectives of emotion, refers to the speaker's (or, in questions, the addressee's) state of being glad and does not normally take third-person subjects, whereas *yorokobu,* as a rule, describes a third person's feeling glad and expressing it by speech, attitude, or behavior. Thus, of the following examples, (1) is correct, but (2) is not.

(1) **Kodomo wa yasumi ni naru to yorokobu.**

Children are glad when a holiday arrives.

(2) **Watashi wa yasumi ni naru to yorokobu.*

I am glad when a holiday arrives.

In (2), to express the idea intended, *yorokobu* would have to be replaced by *ureshii,* as in

(3) **Watashi wa yasumi ni naru to ureshii.**

I am glad when a holiday arrives.

Yorokonde, the gerund form of *yorokobu,* however, may be used in reference to any subject, even the speaker.

(4) **Yorokonde ukagaimasu.**

I'll be glad to come [to your place]. (lit., I'll come rejoicingly.)

YOROSHIKU よろしく **lit., suitably, favorably, kindly**

When you wish to ask someone to convey your regards to someone else, there are many ways to express that idea in

English, such as "Remember me to so-and-so," "Give so-and-so my regards," "Say hello to so-and-so," etc. In Japanese, on the other hand, there is basically only one formula: *daredare* (so-and-so) *ni yoroshiku.*

(1) **Okusan ni yoroshiku.**

Please remember me (lit., [remember me] suitably) to your wife.

Japanese speakers are probably more greeting conscious than English speakers and therefore use this formula more frequently than the latter do similar English expressions.

Yoroshiku is also a greeting exchanged between two people when introduced to each other for the first time. In this case, *yoroshiku* is usually preceded by *doozo* (see DOOZO).

(2) **Doozo yoroshiku.**

How do you do? (lit., Please [treat me] favorably.)

Yoroshiku is also used when requesting that someone take care of something or someone for you. In this case, the word expressing the thing or person concerned is followed by the particle *o,* as in

(3) **Musuko o yoroshiku onegai-shimasu.**

lit., Please take care of my son kindly.

This sentence can be used, for instance, when you are talking to a teacher who is just beginning to teach your son. In a similar situation, English-speaking parents might occasionally make a request such as "Please be tough with my son," but they are probably more likely to say something like "I hope my son will do all right." Japanese speakers seem more request oriented than English speakers.

YUBI 指 finger, toe

English-speaking students of Japanese usually equate *yubi*

with "finger," but *yubi* actually has a much broader range of meaning than "finger" because it may also refer to toes. Although English speakers conceive of fingers and toes as totally unrelated to each other and have two entirely different terms referring to them, Japanese speakers conceive of both as belonging to the same category and have one term for both. When it is absolutely necessary to make a distinction, however, one can do so by saying *te no yubi* (lit., "hand *yubi*") and *ashi no yubi* (lit., "foot *yubi*"), as in

(1) **Ashi no yubi wa te no yubi yori futokute mijikai.**
      Toes are thicker and shorter than fingers.

   In English, despite the fact that one can say "There are five fingers on each hand" or "Each hand has five fingers," one does not normally refer to a thumb as a finger (Ogasawara, p. 122). In Japanese, on the other hand, one can point to one's thumb and say, for example,

(2) **Kono yubi ga itai n desu.**
      This finger hurts.

In English, one would probably say in such a case

(3) My thumb hurts.

YUKKURI ゆっくり **slowly**

Yukkuri means "slow" or "slowly."

(1) **Mada hayai kara yukkuri arukimashoo.**
      It's still early; let's walk more slowly.

   There is another word meaning "slow," *osoi* (see OSOI). In (2) below, both (a) and (b) mean "He eats slowly" (lit., "His way of eating is slow").

(2) **Ano hito wa tabekata ga** |(a) **osoi.**
                                   |(b) **yukkuri da.**

There is, however, a slight difference between (2a) and

(2b). While (2a) simply means "He eats slowly," (2b) implies more because *yukkuri* connotes "in a relaxed, leisurely manner." This meaning of *yukkuri* becomes more apparent in the following example:

(3) **Kinoo wa kaisha ga yasumi datta kara, ichi-nichi yuk-kuri yasunda.**

Yesterday I took it easy (lit., rested relaxedly) all day, since I had the day off from work.

Yukkuri-suru (lit., "to do something slowly") is regularly used in the sense of "to take it easy" or "to relax," especially in the often used invitation *Yukkuri-shite kudasai* meaning "Please stay longer" or "Make yourself at home." A politer version of *Yukkuri-shite kudasai* is *Goyukkuri-nasatte kudasai,* which is frequently shortened to *Goyukkuri.*

YUUGATA 夕方 dusk

Although *yuugata* is usually equated with English "evening," *yuugata* is actually earlier than evening, and shorter as well. It is from about half past four to six or so, about the time Japanese wives are busy preparing dinner. The word *yuugata* evokes a certain picture in most Japanese people's minds: children going home for dinner after having played outside, birds flying home to roost, and the sun about to set in the west. The after-dinner hours are normally not referred to as *yuugata.*

YUUMEI 有名 famous

To express the idea of "famous for something," use *de yuumei.*

(1) **Kamakura wa daibutsu de yuumei desu.**

Kamakura is famous for its great statue of Buddha.

To express the idea of "famous as something," however, use *to shite yuumei* instead.

(2) **Kamakura wa daibutsu no aru machi to shite** (not **de*) **yuumei desu.**

Kamakura is famous as a city with a great statue of Buddha.

To shite is not as conversational as *de,* however. Although (1) and (2) basically say the same thing, (1) is better suited to conversation, and (2) to writing.

┌ ┐
ZANNEN 残念 regret

Zannen "regret" literally means "lingering thought." In other words, it refers to the sense of sorrowful dissatisfaction that lingers on in the mind of someone who realizes that things did not or are not going to turn out according to his wish.

(1) **Araki-san ga issho ni ikarenakute zannen desu.**

It's too bad Mr. Araki can't go with us.

(2) **Zannen desu ga pikunikku wa toriyame ni narimashita.**

I am sorry but the picnic has been canceled.

Zannen should not be used when you feel a sense of guilt about something bad that you have done. For that use *kookai-suru* (see KOOKAI).

(3) **Ano hito no okane o nusunda koto o**

> (a) **zannen ni omou.*
> (b) **kookai-shite-iru.**

By the same token, do not use *zannen* as an expression of apology. Unlike English "I am sorry," which may be used either as a plain expression of regret (as in the English translation of example 2 above) or as a form of apology (as in "I am sorry I lost your pen"), *zannen* cannot be used for an apology. For that purpose, use *Mooshiwake arimasen* "I don't know how to apologize," *Shitsurei-shimashita* "I'm sorry for what I've done," *Sumimasen* "I'm sorry."

ZENZEN 全然 [not] at all

Zenzen, as a rule, is used only in negative environments.
(1) **Zenzen wakarimasen.**
     I don't understand at all.
(2) **Zenzen muzukashiku arimasen.**
     It's not at all difficult.
  Zenzen is also used with words of negative orientation (though they are not negative in form). In this case, the English equivalent is "completely."
(3) **Zenzen chigaimasu.**
     It's completely wrong (*or* different).
(4) **Zenzen shippai da.**
     It failed completely.
  In informal conversation, *zenzen* is sometimes used as an intensifier with the meaning of "very," as in
(5) **zenzen ii**
     very good
This last use, however, is rather slangy and is not recommended.

ZUIBUN ずいぶん very, quite, a lot

Zuibun as an intensifier is often quite similar in meaning to *totemo* "very."

(1) **Kinoo wa zuibun** (or **totemo**) **atsukatta.**
     Yesterday was very hot.
(2) **Nihon wa gasorin ga zuibun** (or **totemo**) **takai.**
     In Japan, gasoline is very expensive.

Jorden (1, p. 117) points out that *zuibun* and *totemo* have different distributions. For example, whereas both *zuibun* and *totemo* occur before *takai* "high, expensive," only *totemo* can occur before *ii* "good."

Zuibun perhaps reflects the speaker's sentiment or subjective judgment while *totemo* does not. For example, in (1) and (2) above, the versions with *totemo* seem like objective statements whereas the versions with *zuibun* seem to imply the speaker's surprise, disgust, etc.

It is probably because of this subjective implication that in exclamations such as (3) below, *zuibun* is more appropriate than *totemo*.

(3) (a) **Zuibun** | **ookiku natta nee.**
     (b) *?Totemo* |
         How you've grown! (lit., How big you've gotten!)

BIBLIOGRAPHY

Bunka-cho (Agency for Cultural Affairs). *Gaikokujin no tame no Kihongo Yorei Jiten* (A Dictionary of Basic Words for Foreigners). Tokyo: Bunka-cho, 1971.

Hattori, Shiro. *Eigo Kiso-goi no Kenkyu* (A Study in the Basic Vocabulary of English). Tokyo: Sanseido, 1968.

Ikegami, Yoshihiko. *Imi no Sekai* (The World of Meaning). Tokyo: Nihon Hoso Shuppan Kyokai, 1978.

Jorden, Eleanor Harz. *Beginning Japanese*. 2 vols. New Haven and London: Yale University Press, 1963.

Keene, Donald. *"Nihongo no Muzukashisa"* (The Difficulty of Japanese). In *Watashi no Gaikokugo* (My Foreign Language), edited by Tadao Umesao and Michio Nagai, pp. 154–63. Tokyo: Chuokoronsha, 1970.

Kindaichi, Haruhiko, ed. *Meikai Nihongo Akusento Jiten* (A Clearly Explained Dictionary of Japanese Accent), 6th ed. Tokyo; Sanseido, 1962.

Kunihiro, Tetsuya. *Kozoteki Imiron* (Structural Semantics). Tokyo: Sanseido, 1967.

Kuno, Susumu. *The Structure of the Japanese Language*. Cambridge, Mass., and London: MIT Press, 1973.

Kurokawa, Shozo. *Nihongo to Eigo no Aida* (Between Japanese and English). Tokyo: Natsumesha, 1978.

Maruya, Saiichi. *Nihongo no tame ni* (For the Japanese Language). Tokyo: Shinchosha, 1974.

Matsui, Emi. *Eisakubun ni okeru Nihonjinteki Ayamari* (Japanese-like Errors in English). Tokyo: Taishukan, 1979.

Matsuo, Hirou, et al. *Ruigigo no Kenkyu* (A Study of Synonyms). Report no. 28 by Kokuritsu Kokugo Kenkyujo (The National Language Research Institute). Tokyo: Shuei Shuppan, 1965.

Miura, Akira, *English Loanwords: A Selection.* Tokyo and Rutland, Vt.: Charles E. Tuttle, 1979.

Miyoshi, Hiroshi. *Nichi–Ei Kotoba no Chigai* (Differences Between Japanese and English Expressions). Tokyo: Koronsha, 1978.

Mizutani, Osamu, and Mizutani, Nobuko. *Nihongo Notes,* 1. Tokyo: The Japan Times, 1977.

———. *Nihongo Notes,* 2. Tokyo: The Japan Times, 1979.

Morita, Yoshiyuki. *Kiso Nihongo* (Basic Japanese). Tokyo: Kadokawa Shoten, 1977.

Ogasawara, Rinju. *"Eigo-jisho to Nichi–Ei Goi no Hikaku"* (A Comparison of the Japanese and English Vocabularies Through English-Language Dictionaries). In *Nichi–Eigo no Hikaku* (A Comparison of Japanese and English), edited by Kenkyusha, pp. 115–39. Tokyo: Kenkyusha, 1978.

Ohno, Susumu, and Shibata, Takeshi, eds. *Goi to Imi* (Words and Meanings). *Iwanami Koza: Nihongo* (Iwanami Course: The Japanese Language), 9. Tokyo: Iwanami Shoten, 1977.

Sandness, Karen. "The Use of *Kare* and *Kanojo." Journal of the Association of Teachers of Japanese* 10, no. 1 (March 1975), pp. 75–86.

Shibata, Takeshi. *"Ikite-iru Hogen"* (Living Dialects). In *Modern Japanese for University Students,* 2, 3rd ed., compiled by the Japanese Department, International Christian University, pp. 20–25. Tokyo: International Christian University, 1970.

Shibata, Takeshi, et al. *Kotoba no Imi* (The Meanings of Words), 2. Tokyo: Heibonsha, 1979.

Soga, Matsuo, and Matsumoto, Noriko. *Foundations of Japanese Language.* Tokyo: Taishukan, 1978.

Suzuki, Takao. *Japanese and the Japanese*. Translated by Akira Miura. Tokyo, New York, and San Francisco: Kodansha International, 1978.

Tokugawa, Munemasa, and Miyajima, Tatsuo. *Ruigigo Jiten* (A Dictionary of Synonyms). Tokyo: Tokyodo, 1962.

Yanafu, Akira. *Hon'yaku to wa Nani ka* (What Is Translation?). Tokyo: Hosei University Press, 1976.

INDEX

This index includes all the main entries as well as a few hundred more words and expressions that appear in the text explanations. The main entries are in boldface type while the other words are in regular type. Page numbers in boldface type show where the words appear as main entries.